How to Hire
(or Fire) Your
Financial
Advisor

How to **Hire** (or **Fire**) Your Financial Advisor

Ten Simple Questions to Guide Decision Making

Ivan M. Illán, CFS

HOW TO HIRE (OR FIRE) YOUR FINANCIAL ADVISOR
TEN SIMPLE QUESTIONS TO GUIDE DECISION MAKING

iUniverse books may be ordered through booksellers or by contacting:

iUniverse
1663 Liberty Drive
Bloomington, IN 47403
www.iuniverse.com
1-800-Authors (1-800-288-4677)

Because of the dynamic nature of the Internet, any web addresses or links contained in this book may have changed since publication and may no longer be valid. The views expressed in this work are solely those of the author and do not necessarily reflect the views of the publisher, and the publisher hereby disclaims any responsibility for them.

Any people depicted in stock imagery provided by Thinkstock are models, and such images are being used for illustrative purposes only. Certain stock imagery © Thinkstock.

ISBN: 978-1-4917-7018-4 (sc)
ISBN: 978-1-4917-7036-8 (hc)
ISBN: 978-1-4917-7017-7 (e)

Library of Congress Control Number: 2015910697

Print information available on the last page.

iUniverse rev. date: 08/31/2015

How to Hire (or Fire) Your Financial Advisor Disclaimer

This book seeks to provide fair and objective perspective on the subject of the asset management industry. There are many stories and anecdotes that are based on true experiences, and the names of people and firms involved have been excluded except where condition of privacy is not necessary. The Author is not engaged in the dissemination or rendering of legal, accounting, or other professional advisory services by publishing this book. Since every individual circumstance is unique, the Reader is encouraged to seek the counsel and advice of those professionals to provide the most relevant and appropriate guidance for their situation. The Author disclaims any liability, loss or risk which is incurred as a consequence of the use and application of any of the contents of this work.

To my abuelo, the champion economist and my first mentor

CONTENTS

INTRODUCTION

What if a conductor in the employ of a symphony orchestra could only play the specific notes that were board approved or preferred—or that simply paid him better than other notes? The result would be discord, dissonance, and cacophony, a true disservice. This short book expands on the idea that the best retail investing experience can be derived only from a harmonious, conflict-free conductor—as the subject of this book, a financial advisor (FA). There are two other main themes that are included herein and the subject of much regulatory scrutiny nowadays: (1) suitability- and (2) fiduciary-care standards.

In short, most retail investors work with an FA who is subject to a suitability-care standard. This means that as long as the product recommendation is deemed suitable based on the client's goals and objectives in that specific moment in time, the sale is said to be appropriate. A fiduciary standard, by contrast, involves no product sale but rather an ongoing duty to make recommendations and portfolio changes that are only in the client's best interest. We'll explore this dichotomy in the chapters ahead. Most of this book discusses *why* you should conduct a qualitative audit of a financial advisor's recommendations. If you want the quick review on *how*, skip directly to chapter 9 or the checklist at the end of this book.

This book is part memoir and part discourse on my twenty years on both the institutional and retail sides of the asset management and financial product distribution industry, in order to provide education and overall insight on how this industry really functions. I want readers to understand enough about how this industry functions to be able to select an FA who will work in their best interests. The title of this book suggests a revealing opinion about the said industry. It's not enough to know how to hire an FA; you also need to know when and why one might need to be fired and replaced. Also, it's probably best to review the glossary at the back of this book first, to familiarize yourself with the variety of terms used and introduced throughout.

Frankly, I wish a book like this would not be needed in the marketplace, but it is now certainly required reading. I've worked as a key executive at some of the largest financial product manufacturing companies and in partnership with the biggest financial product distributors in the United States. I've witnessed firsthand how investment banking and financial product distribution channels truly function—and it's not pretty. During this experience of "working in the kitchen," I came to loathe the advisor greed, managerial product pushing, ethics void, and generally putrid "let's put some lipstick on this pig" mentality that permeates the industry. The goal of this story is to shift your perspective, however slightly, away from the product-pushing game and toward a philosophy of personal wealth and investment stewardship. In short, I hope to give you tools that empower you to question those who seek to give you financial advice.

If you are a professional advisor (e.g., CPA, attorney, insurance agent, or registered representative), the message of this story is vital to you—that there's a need to demand a higher care standard in the financial advisory industry. Each professional advisor can choose to conduct his or her business accordingly and serve *all* clients with solely *the client's* interest at heart.

My story shows the inner workings of the financial world, and while a biography is a bit unusual in this type of book, it's necessary so you can see how the financial-services world works and choose an FA who works in your best interest.

In this book I'll offer the retail investor information by "pulling back the curtain" and provide background information concerning the various regulatory standards of care available. There are no specific financial strategies, companies, platforms, services, or products advocated here. The fact stands that every individual has unique circumstances and conditions to achieve wealth preservation, income generation, or growth goals. For financial-services professionals, this book will share the best practices in providing a higher standard of care. At the same time, for the retail investor, I aim to broaden the knowledge base by which you evaluate and hold accountable your current financial advisory relationships.

CHAPTER ONE

My Early Economic Interests and Career

I grew up as the son of two immigrants, and I was raised like many first-generation Americans. My parents encouraged me to be inquisitive and fostered an entrepreneurial spirit.

The one constant in my youth was my paternal grandfather. He lived (and still lives at age ninety-one) in Miami Beach, Florida. Every summer I would spend a number of months with him. His stories were endless. His opinions were varied, intense, and polarizing to others who found themselves in conversation with him. His acerbic and challenging persona is due, in my opinion, to who he was during his life in Cuba.

My grandfather José M. Illán was the former undersecretary of the treasury for the Castro revolutionary government established in 1959. "He was a member of the first cabinet of the Castro government and collaborated in good faith, with an administration which he believed would mark the beginning of an era patriotic and [filled with] honest rectifications."[1] His stories of Ernesto "Che" Guevara and Fidel Castro were mesmerizing.

I recall one story where, after he discovered that Castro was not planning on returning political power to a democracy, my grandfather was presented with a most dire situation. Both Che and Castro had already begun installing cabinet members who were not going to challenge their newly found authority; however, my grandfather's reputation as a former president of the Catholic Youth Organization in Cuba and a staunch anti-Communist with pro-capitalist writings would have to be dealt with, either through coercion or death.

One afternoon he was called into a meeting with Che after the Minister of Finance nervously declined the invitation to the meeting with the "Comandante." Che and my grandfather began a back-and-forth conversation, in which Che provided a heated tirade of why new reforms needed to be put in place and why these reforms were in the best interest of the Cuban economy and its people.

My grandfather did not agree, and the argument escalated. "After all," says my grandfather, "he was armed with a gun. I had only a pen."

Perhaps in that moment, my grandfather's resolve was fashioned and his future secured as a foremost authority on the economic harm that would beset Cuba under the Castro regime. My grandfather politely, calmly told Che a series of

---

[1] Jose M. Illán, *Cuba: Facts & Figures of an Economy in Ruins 1902–1963*, 1st ed. in English (Miami, FL: July 1964)—my grandfather's seminal publication on the subject. This citation is from the publisher, from the back cover.

placating items that could be drafted. Che, confounded by the agreeable response, asked my grandfather whether the Minister of Finance would sign these proposed policies that they had just hatched on the spot.

"Most certainly," he answered, knowing full well his boss would sign if he wanted to remain free, or worse, avoid the firing squad.

My grandfather left the meeting convinced that he would be joining his fellow revolutionary government "obstacles" in the dungeons, or that he would have a black hood thrown over his head on a morning commute or his home riddled with bullets. He told my grandmother they were in trouble and to prepare for the worst. Their three sons, one being my father, were kept unaware of the impending danger.

My grandfather already had been told by secretarial staffers that his name was, in fact, on the revolutionary government's communication that contained hundreds of other names. He met again with the Minister of Finance days later and laid into him. "I know I'm on the list," he said, referring to those who opposed the revolution's programs and who were disappearing one by one. "I know I'm next, and I don't intend on living in fear, so just arrest me now," he sternly demanded.

The cabinet member calmly replied, "I have no idea what you're referring to, Sr. Illán; there's no list."

Meanwhile, my grandfather had already made plans to leave Havana for Madrid, where he had already begun to seek new employment and could be safe with his family. Within a couple of days, he was back with the Minister of Finance. Appealing to his boss's honor as a former military man, Illán sweetly stated, "I know you will allow me to leave Habana without complication, since you are an honorable man." The approach worked, as apparently the minister was caught off guard; he agreed there would be no arrest if my grandfather and his family made an attempt to leave Cuba. A car followed my grandfather home and followed the family to the airport. Three sons, my grandfather and his wife, and a few suitcases all escaped from Cuba that night.

My grandfather's career evolved later into a senior leadership role within the Inter-American Development Bank, the largest source of development financing for Latin America and the Caribbean, established in 1959. He was a frequent guest of *Radio Marti*, an author of several anti-Castro books and hundreds of articles, and a contributing columnist to the *Miami Herald* for many years. His ethical and moral imperatives on the good of an economy being driven by free-market capitalism were his hallmark.

As I think back to these early stories, mixed with the personal passion with which he presented his ideas, it's no wonder why my own curiosities turned to the financial world. A young six-year-old boy hearing about his grandfather being threatened and nearly murdered for simply *not* signing his name to documents that would have negative economic impact on the lives of millions of people is a great big idea for a kid. It was an idea that seemingly burrowed deep into my consciousness, creating immovable pillars of moral and ethical certitude. If he was willing to die for his ideas, I figured economics *must* be *that* important.

This root philosophy went far beyond the intellectual

banter that accompanied our family dinner table concerning currency devaluation or budget deficits. His experience taught me later that not knowing whether an industry will embrace or ignore your message is irrelevant; making the effort without regret and holding nothing back to fight for your ideals is the test of courage and what it means to be truly revolutionary.

I learned from Sr. José M. Illán, *mi abuelo,* my grandfather, that you can be comfortable with what you know, lulled into a state of trance by the world around you, only to be rudely awakened by a clamoring panic-stricken world. For that six-year-old boy, the perspective he gave me was unique and powerful. So much so, that I started to do my own research in an effort to find a fairer, brighter accounting of the frightful, brutal, dog-eat-dog socioeconomic world he described.

By age twelve my mornings began with in-depth reads of *The Wall Street Journal* and routine ordering of the annual reports from New York Stock Exchange (NYSE)-listed companies. The dramatic and crazy world of tyrannical political and business despots became increasingly fascinating to me. It was then I figured I couldn't do worse than other folks, so maybe I should take a hand at investing, or more accurately in hindsight, the now-termed "day-trading," hardly actual investing, as it's rather more akin to speculation and gambling—more on investing as gambling later.

After all, my father hadn't the time or inclination to invest my college fund, so I asked him to allow me to manage it. There was less than $10,000 total, and his response in his typical, engineering logician mode was, "Sure, but if you lose it, you go to community college."

By the time I was fifteen years old, there were certain days I was making as much money per diem as my father was by day-trading stocks and open-end mutual fund shares. When it came time, I had the supplemental funds available for college. After declining a Presidential Scholarship offer from New York University's Stern School of Business, I attended Boston College on an academic scholarship and grants and earned two distinct degrees (BS, Finance and BA, Philosophy), which satisfied my bargain-seeking mind in getting a two-for-one deal.

As I embarked on postgraduate life in the "real world," I kept my passion for finance ever at the forefront of my mind.

LEARNING THE BUSINESS AND DISCOVERING FLAWS

I made my way to the Windy City to begin my formal career in the investment world. I knew no one, nor had any prior connection to the area. I discovered a temporary job in Chicago with an employer who had legendary success in financial product development and distribution. I've omitted the company name, but in reality, all money-management firms that seek to distribute their products through distribution channels engage in the kinds of activities I describe.

I interviewed for the position, and he offered me the job on the spot, and with it a foothold into the secretive, clubby world of investment bankers, money management, and brokerage firms. To clarify, this particular investment-management firm was quite different from others, as it did not rely upon its own proprietary sales force for retail distribution as most investment-banking shops do—like the ones you see set up like stores in your neighborhoods saying "put your money in here," such as commonplace banks, brokerage shops, and so on. In my opinion this factor played a role in its leadership in product development innovation over retail investment-banking shops, due to meeting the continuous product distribution needs of institutional distribution channel clients. That being said, developing new investment products (known as product manufacturing), like mutual funds or exchange-traded funds, was done in partnership with the distribution channels. These channels needed to buy into the design concept and strategy offering so that the new product launch would be a successful one for all the institutions involved.

I had yet to learn that a primary conflict in financial product distribution lies within the financial advisor's "education" from the asset-management companies' wholesalers. This creates a conflict because the education is not unbiased. The FA is far less sophisticated than any chief investment officer managing many hundreds of billions of dollars, so how does the FA have the true intelligence to evaluate the situation? If FAs did, wouldn't they be the ones running the many billions? For now it was up to me to figure out how to climb the proverbial ladder. You cannot even conceive of industry change unless you first learn all the areas that need improvement.

So each day I set out to understand the needs of the wholesaling personnel at my new employer. I did so by asking questions or conducting informal sales-force surveys, but always with the intent to add discernible value to the firm. National sales support became my lifeblood and a foundation to the unique experience and perspective I've since come to acquire. I figured the better the information and education conveyed to FAs and branch managers from our firm, the better retail investor portfolio construction would result—using our company's financial products, of course. Adding value in this way is now a common strategy in how money managers win mindshare and asset flows among their client advisors.

I thrived in the asset-management business, guiding its institutional client reporting innovation. By 2000 I had worked for four years in the investment product distribution machine of one of the most successful financial product manufacturing firms in the United States. This company is still credited with being an early manufacturer of unit investment trusts (UITs) and closed-end funds (CEFs). The CEF product spawned the varied exchange-traded fund marketplace today, representing an ever-growing allocation of an investor's dollars. I achieved many accolades during my tenure, including being part of the team that had an NYSE record-breaking IPO for the largest state municipal CEF listing ever—which still stands today. Moving into a frontline wholesaling position proved very educational. My time there was without a doubt an enriching, mentored experience that set me on the path I find myself on today nearly twenty years later. Much of the balance of this book shares observations made during this time in my career.

By the age of twenty-five, I felt I had learned all there was to learn from my first employer. I started to look outward for something different, and thus began my next career phase. Having made structural innovations at a corporate level, this became my catalyst as an early adopter and promoter of innovative investment products. But what I have come to learn is that no amount of product innovation truly benefits retail investors, or at least, not for very long. This is the decisive precursor to understanding the disadvantages faced by most retail investors, who are "sold" product that they simply do not need.

One of the best examples of this was the debacle that was the Munder NetNet Fund. The wholesaling force of Munder Capital Management aggressively told the story of this innovative product offering that was going to take advantage of all the opportunities for wealth creation in the Internet. The fund grew to $11 billion in assets under management (AUM) in 2000, but by late 2001 had only $1 billion in assets due to the dot-com crash and resulting investor redemptions.[2]

At this time I wanted to parlay my experience in investment product distribution and broker/dealer syndicate building into a more boutique career. So in 2000 I went ahead and founded MingConsulting Inc. as an investment banking consultancy firm to guide the distribution channel sales of asset-management companies. However, the challenge of finding investment firms that were interested in hiring a midtwenties-aged consultant was no easy task.

---

[2] Diya Gullapalli, "A Fund That May Be Unforgettable: Pummeled Munder NetNet Haunts Firm's Turnaround," *Wall Street Journal*, October 3, 2006, http://online.wsj.com/articles/SB115921512811973383.

STOCK JUNGLE: THE FICKLE NATURE
OF FINANCIAL PRODUCTS

Luckily technology was accommodating of youth, and through a head-hunting website, I discovered a consultant position that sounded as if it had been written for me. The company was a recently organized SEC-regulated registered investment advisor, and they were in search of a director of sales. The name of the firm was StockJungle.com Investment Advisors, Inc., and its Community Intelligence Fund had a year-to-date October 21, 2000, return of positive 21.4 percent versus an average negative 6.04 percent for other large-cap growth funds in the United States.[3] The mutual-fund family had a grand total of three funds, all based upon a sophisticated algorithm that essentially boiled down the holdings from a community of fifty thousand online traders who ran fictional portfolios.

The idea was instantly compelling, and in the heat of the new dot-com economy, the desire to affiliate with such a wildly innovative idea was a tremendous draw. Soon after meeting with the founder, I was offered the position of vice president, director of sales, and immediately set about establishing a full distribution and sales plan that would provide maximum exposure and leverage financial advisors.

After mounting a comprehensive dog and pony show crisscrossing the United States for more than a year, sales were still stagnant by my expectations. The financial journalists

---

[3] Stacy Forster, "InteractiveFunds, iExchange Merge, Plan a Mutual Fund," *Wall Street Journal*, October 22, 2000, http://www.wsj.com/articles/SB971969080654210587.

had a merry time poking fun at the idea that a bunch of online traders could provide any kind of data worth analyzing, and in doing so, inadvertently made our "stock" go way up. The attention garnered had several acquisition offers from other financial websites. My net worth on paper (due to stock options) was more than $5 million, mentally rewarding but hardly a victory—it was only meaningless paper wealth. I was far more interested in achieving the goals I had set in the business plan when I first started working with StockJungle.com.

However, the negativity highlighted by financial journalists won out. In hindsight this makes plenty of sense. The primary advertising revenue source for financial publications comes from established money-management firms and brokerage houses, neither of which were part of this egalitarian product design, which was fixated on reduced fees and elimination of distribution conflicts of interests.

On April 2, 2001, a front-page Money & Investing Section article in the *Wall Street Journal*, with a snazzy title of "Online 'Community' Funds Aren't Finding Much Support,"[4] was published. The article was replete with an embarrassing cartoon representation of five shocked online traders linked through extension cords to a printer with a piece of paper streaming from it with the words "community investment fund" and a chart with an arrow pointing down. This certainly was my final indication to start looking for my next job.

Anecdotally, precisely ten years later to the month,

---

[4] Tom Lauricella, "Online 'Community' Funds Aren't Finding Much Support," *Wall Street Journal*, April 2, 2001, C1, http://www.wsj.com/articles/ SB986164214781499677.

a scholarly article published in the *International Journal of Electronic Commerce* entitled "Expert Stock Picker: The Wisdom of (Experts in) Crowds,"[5] coauthored by Shawndra Hill at the Wharton School, University of Pennsylvania, and Noah Ready-Campbell, former associate product manager at Google, provided some welcome, though late, vindication. The article's abstract states:

> The wealth and richness of user-generated content may enable firms and individuals to aggregate consumer-think for better business understanding ... Our method allows us to identify and rank "experts" within the crowd, enabling better stock pick decisions than the S&P 500. We show that the online crowd performs better, on average, than the S&P 500 for two test time periods, 2008 and 2009, in terms of both overall returns and risk-adjusted returns, as measured by the Sharpe ratio.

This history illustrates that an idea panned at one time can be lauded in another and financial markets and the resulting products offered in them are fickle at best.

Unfortunately, StockJungle.com shuttered its doors within three months of the 2001 *Wall Street Journal* article. I

---

5   Shawndra Hill and Noah Ready-Campbell, "Expert Stock Picker: The Wisdom of (Experts in) Crowds," *International Journal of Electronic Commerce* 15, no. 3 (Spring 2011): 73–102, http://www.researchgate.net/publication/228403831_Expert_Stock_Picker_The_Wisdom_of_(Experts_in)_Crowds.

had already been searching for another opportunity since its publication—perhaps this time, something not *so* innovative.

LESSON OF 9/11: FEAR SELLS

Within a few weeks, a money-management firm based in Toronto (with operations in Calgary and Vancouver) found me, and I was excited to be in their employ. This company had been (and continues to be) a leading financial product manufacturer, with established distribution channels within the Canadian financial intermediary marketplace. Its sister company had been running the largest and most successful Canadian royalty trust in the marketplace for some time.

I had secured a consulting agreement with both enterprises, albeit with varied goals and objectives for each entity. The first order of business was to secure significant secondary market support for their flagship closed-end fund. Success in this endeavor was measured in how many additional FAs were engaged in trading this security, as well as overall daily trading volume increase of its shares on the AMEX. The timing of this initiative's launch was, and still is, haunting.

Then 9/11 happened.

Global markets, in particular energy markets, were in disarray. On a prior occasion, the firm had hired the speaker services of the former director of the US Central Intelligence Agency, Robert Gates. They saw an opportunity to utilize his perspective once again to help the advisor community digest the scope and gravity of the attack.

Within a week of 9/11, we produced a "What Happens Now?" presentation to more than three hundred FAs in the

Los Angeles mega-complex of a major wire-house brokerage firm. The Director Gates presentation would come at the cost of a five-minute commercial opportunity just prior to the presentation. Some may argue, as I did, that this was vital perspective for FAs to share with their clients. However, I now believe it is not just bad taste but morally and ethically wrong to use any event of such devastation as an opportunity to sell or position products in the marketplace.

The firm's goal, however, had been realized, as the secondary market float for this oil and gas royalty trust saw a 300 percent increase in AMEX trading volume for years after. The 9/11 tragedy being used as a tool to jockey for product visibility within the FA community is not an isolated incident. Every day, financial advisors, brokerage firms, and money-management companies disseminate communications that play upon the fear and greed emotions that retail investors use as primary decision-making drivers.

Instead, what investors need is to be guided through a logical plan.[6] Any good financial plan is rooted in identifying goals, needs, and objectives of the investor. These inputs, coupled with a sense of investor risk tolerance, should guide the portfolio design. Most investors do not buy mutual funds with a governing plan because they were sold on historical performance, which many studies have shown has little

---

[6] Zach Anchors, "Table Gets Turned on a Panicked Client," Dow Jones Newswires, July 14, 2011, http://www.alignewealth.com/new/alignewealth/PracticeMgmt_DowJonesSMALL.pdf?advisorid=4022370.

statistical relevance to future performance.[7] Investors should spend more time developing an understanding of their own needs and objectives.

MONEY-MANAGEMENT INDUSTRY TAKES CARE OF ITSELF

The next project came from the firm's sister company. They had tremendous success distributing closed-end funds (CEFs) through the Canadian FA market. They created a certain kind of equity hedging strategy within a closed-end fund structure. I spent more than a year traveling around the United States (e.g., LA, NY, Honolulu, Seattle, Portland, San Diego, Phoenix, Dallas, Denver, Chicago, Atlanta, Memphis, Birmingham, and Tampa) presenting to the investment bankers and advisors at smaller regional broker/dealer firms, seeking their distribution partnership through their FA channels.

However, even though the syndicate of broker/dealers I had successfully secured had committed 70 percent of the target capital size (the product sponsor had a $50 million Series 1 asset target), I ultimately failed to secure their innovative covered-call writing closed-end product to list on the AMEX or NYSE. The CEO wanted to meet target, and if that couldn't be done, we'd just pull the offering altogether. This was an erroneous judgment (in my then estimation). But upon further consideration, it was probably best, since my first employer had already begun product development work on

---

[7] Christopher B. Philips, CFA, and Francis M. Kinniry Jr., CFA, "Mutual Fund Ratings and Future Performance," Vanguard Research, June 2010, http://www.vanguard.com/pdf/icrwmf.pdf.

their own similar offering, having been inspired by this new idea. There's no way my client could have competed in the marketplace with such a dominant market competitor.

In the competitive world of financial product launches, I learned a lesson firsthand, since my first employer had begun development almost as soon as I introduced the strategy to them for a possible joint venture with the company that I'd been consulting. This failure to launch had left me empty-handed, both emotionally and financially. I had my fill of the institutional games. Financial product distribution is all about taking care of numero uno, the money-management firm that sells its products to investors and pays brokers for the access.

The best example of how the money-management industry has taken care of itself is the proliferation of ETFs.[8] Exchange-traded funds and their cousins, closed-end funds, are underwritten through a syndicate of broker/dealers and sponsored by the money-management firm. Both the money-management firm and the broker/dealer make big money when such a product is actually listed on the NYSE or AMEX, and then there are the ongoing internal expense ratio and fees afterward. Once listed, the investors cannot redeem their shares as with open-end mutual funds. Instead, investors must sell their shares on the exchange to another investor willing to buy. The money managers never have to concern themselves again with pesky investors who sell at inopportune times, also known in the industry as "managing to redemptions." Money

[8] Anna Bernasek, "Choices Abound in an E.T.F. Boom," *New York Times*, July 12, 2014, http://www.nytimes.com/2014/07/13/business/mutfund/choices-abound-in-an-etf-boom.html?_r=0.

managers view this type of product as evergreen income, since the investor cannot ever pull the money away from the firm, and the firm collects its fund expenses and fees forever.

My contract had swiftly come to a close, and yet again I found myself on the search for a meaningful engagement with the financial-services industry.

SEEKING PURPOSE AND ETHICS IN FINANCE

Having opened my mind to the possibilities of good ideas residing in the international ethos, I had a desire to further involve myself in international markets and hopped on a plane to Buenos Aires and then Shanghai to see what product development or distribution intelligence I could collect that might be of value to the firms I had done business with prior.

As it turned out, no one had any interest in South America or China at the time (early 2000s), at least from a retail financial product distribution standpoint. Today this is very much at the forefront for many financial institutions.

At that time the local markets were, and still are, significantly less sophisticated than the US retail investing public. For example, while in China, I visited various state-owned brokerage houses and watched as folks sat in their chairs, eyes glazed over, as the ticker tape of myriad Shanghai stock exchange securities crawled past in red LED. Occasionally someone got up, scribbled something, and handed in the order for processing.

My assessment was that early 2000s' China was exactly like the United States of the 1920s, where speculation investing was the prevailing style or strategy of the day, and we know how that worked out, starting with the crash of 1929, followed by the Great Depression. I have no doubt in my mind that China will have its day of reckoning for its engagement in extreme currency manipulation, rigged market policies, and extremely corrupt crony capitalism. The day when the pendulum will swing in the other direction is coming, as it always does.

After I visited China, I initially decided to leave the investment banking and money-management industry. The decision to leave the industry came out of a couple of important acceptances of truth. The first was that the development and distribution of financial products is a business where the clients are not just consumers, but essentially pawns in the game of "this time it's different" marketing.

Though I believe I worked with some of the best financial product manufacturers in North America, there's no way around the endgame. Raise money—$100 million, maybe $1 billion—and then invest it as the marketing described, and *hope* that area of the market invested in stays stable and in demand for a period long enough to show decent out-of-the-gate performance; and then by the time it fails and falters due to normal market cycles, come to market through your distribution channel of FAs to offer a product that can fix the problem put in place by the old strategy.

If I went to a doctor who performed one recommended operation to solve an initial problem I had, and then two years later told me that he'd like an opportunity to perform another operation to fix the prior one, I'd have a great malpractice suit. *Why does this FA behavior get rewarded via additional commissions in new product sales for them and their firms?*

The second reason I left an institutional-sided career was a personal one—a desire to have a purpose-driven life, a purpose not defined by the pursuit of money. Every deal or IPO pays great money ... when, and only when, the deal is closed. The pressure to keep engaging in deals drives a vicious cycle of money mongering. Having that last deal scrapped by a product sponsor for nothing more than their not hitting an arbitrary target left me holding the bag on a year's worth of opportunity cost, all of which was out of my control. I felt betrayed initially, but then liberated.

I vowed that I would not continue in a career where I was *not* in the driver's seat when it came to *quality, ethics,* and *income alignment* with clients.

I consider it a colossal blessing to have experienced the challenges I did, as they set me on a more determined path than I could have ever imagined: a crusade to provide the US retail investor (through better financial-advisor education) a process on how to engage with a true, conflict-free investment advisory service.

CHAPTER TWO

My Career Takes the Road Less Traveled

The epiphany on institutional conflicts of interests had occurred. Seeing firsthand how the goals and objectives for financial-services companies are in direct conflict with the goals and objectives of individual investors, I really had to make a choice. Did I even want to continue a career in the industry at all? Maybe switch gears to accounting or law? I proactively shuttered my own consulting business, even though I was approaching the end of my personal savings. As fate would have it, my savings were bolstered in part from personal real estate investments and stock options exercised during the consultancy work. But those funds would eventually run out.

I was living in China at the time, and I knew it was time for me to seek new employment, but had little hope that I would be able to find something that didn't churn my stomach (not to mention potential clients' accounts). I knew I had to make my way into the retail side of the business from being "on the other side of the desk" as it's said in the industry. I knew I had to work directly with retail investors for the first time in my career—direct benefit and personal impact.

The idea of becoming a financial advisor, like one of the many people I had spent years marketing a myriad of products to to help them make quota so they could keep their jobs to go on to make more money for their firms, was not a joyous or desired career. Frankly, I couldn't imagine it, and when I did it was revolting. However, by the end of my decision making, I knew I had to work doing something in the financial-services industry. Also, I figured my ethical discoveries were not in service to me or anyone else if I ended up in another industry.

As a result I determined the safest, or more aptly less-harmful, route to working with retail clients in the least conflicted manner possible was to find an independent registered investment advisor (RIA) firm. I could use my background to represent their particular investment services directly to clients without an intermediary brokerage house. An RIA firm is a state- or an SEC-registered business that manages money for their clients, typically with $500,000 minimums. There are many thousands of these businesses; most, however, cannot beat their own internally assigned benchmarks.[9] One such RIA firm had opened a conversation with me through an executive-search firm. On the surface this

[9] Chris Flood, "Underperformance Rife Among Active Fund Managers," *Financial Times Limited*, August 24, 2011, http://www.ft.com/intl/cms/s/0/d3b7db8e-ce5e-11e0-99ec-00144feabdc0.html#axzz3ZUTYpFdx.

wasn't very appealing, since it felt like being a cog in a different part of the machine.

I accepted the position of vice president with one of the RIA firms, owned by one of the *Forbes 400 Richest Americans.* The owner was the son of a storied financial guru—one of Warren Buffett's financial mentors. However, this was not the long-term answer I was seeking.

Though I still believed that their investment strategy and process were much better for clients than what I had witnessed in the commissioned, brokerage community, I found an entirely new set of problems. If you were a client who required more comprehensive planning, or perhaps due to your risk tolerance wanted to incorporate guarantees through insurance products to assure yourself of income and liquidity to heirs or wealth-replacement planning, you'd have to go elsewhere since RIAs are not licensed to provide such services.

This highlights yet another challenge in the financial-services industry: the reality that clients become collectors of advisors across a variety of specialties. Who is at the helm guiding the overall planning ... the client? Isn't this the reason why they are hiring all these advisors?[10] Why is there not a single advisor providing advice in a comprehensive fashion? I thought, even if this RIA were to create the most wonderful investment results, if the family's governing documents (e.g., living or family trusts, charitable trusts, family foundations,

---

[10] Kelly Kearsley, "When a Client Has Multiple Financial Advisers," *Wall Street Journal,* December 20, 2013, http://www.wsj.com/articles/SB10001424052 702304367204579270081481758804.

or buyout agreements for closely held family businesses) were poorly drafted or nonexistent, peril increases exponentially. Furthermore, what if the family is not engaged in the conversation of the family's wealth mission statement and values to be clearly transmitted to the next generation? What is the point of having good portfolio returns if the family's money ultimately disappears for all these other more relevant threats? The chance of keeping wealth intact across generations is less than 30 percent, based on accepted industry research.[11]

The statistics surrounding wealth transfer in the United States are abysmal. This loss occurs not from poor investment performance but from spendthrift heirs who never learned how to accept and then manage a windfall. We'll discuss how to address this issue later, but for now the deeper understanding is that even independent RIAs need to provide a comprehensive client solution.

Only months into the position, I felt that this RIA was not the answer, though they were regarded as the largest direct marketer to high net worth households in the world. It's a distinction that is hard to comprehend until you work with their database day in and out, making as many as two hundred to three hundred dials per day, connecting with perhaps fifty people, booking meetings with ten, holding six meetings, and ultimately adding one or two new clients to their roster. During this brief tenure, I gained a tremendous amount of knowledge regarding investor psychology and behavioral finance (a subject I studied initially during my years at Boston

---

[11] Roy Williams and Vic Pressier, *Preparing Heirs* (San Francisco: Robert D. Reed Publishers, 2003).

College). All that being said, their limits to comprehensive financial planning solutions were insurmountable.

LISTENING TO GUT INSTINCT

So, going against everything I stood for but *very* hopeful that I could be different, I accepted a position at a major wirehouse firm in Beverly Hills, a branch I knew very, very well. In fact, that particular office was the top revenue-producing office in the territory that I covered, and in many ways a significant source of my compensation, during my time at my first employer.

I showed up at six thirty on a Monday morning in early 2005. After all, I knew very ethical and respectable reps there. I vowed not to concern myself with the prevailing architecture, distribution, and quota burdens, but rather remain true to the clients' needs and objectives.

So there I was sitting at my desk with all those thoughts knocking around upstairs, and then ... my bowels started in. This is the gut check become manifest. A few restroom visits later, I could not ignore the message my bowels were delivering so very clearly. This place, though I might have the best intentions, bred greed. Even though I was a soldier in this legion with my own daring and evolutionary vision, I would ultimately be powerless in the product distribution fight I started to take on.

I walked into the branch manager's office and told him flatly that I was leaving—"it isn't anything anyone has said or done, but just this isn't the right place for me." He had a blank stare, poor chap—probably thought I was crazy and was glad to be rid of me so soon, avoiding some messy future separation.

As I left the office at nine thirty in the morning, I was excited, delirious, worried, and every other emotion that you'd expect when leaving a stable source of income for the unknown. I was resolved, this time definitively, in the fact that I would make my own decisions based on how I felt about the work I was doing (i.e., the purpose-driven career), not based on the matter of remuneration. I decided to hold myself to a higher standard and concerned myself with how I could benefit society with these experiences and insights. This thinking would shape my next professional chapter. Days, weeks, and months passed without any indication of a new direction. I spoke to more financial-services executive-search folks than I care to recall.

A NEW OPPORTUNITY IN FINANCIAL SERVICES

It was a day just like any other when the call arrived. I picked up the phone to the voice of a managing partner from an agency of a mutually owned life insurance company in Los Angeles. My first response was, "I'm an investment guy. Why would an insurance company be interested in me?" Her response was surprising: "That's why we're calling. We want to talk to you about leading our firm's investment-services division." My interest was piqued, and after another call or two over the next couple of weeks, I began to formulate an idea of what this opportunity might hold.

I was hopeful that working with a minority business

owner (there were few women in field sales leadership roles throughout the financial-services industry) meant my innovative ideas would be accepted because the minority-owned business was outside the business-as-usual mind-set.

A mutual life insurance company is something of a dinosaur in these derivative, hard-charging, quarterly shareholder earning reports times. I was attracted to the premise—a financial-services company that is owned by the very clients that it serves.

For those not familiar with what a mutually owned life insurance company is versus a stock shareholder-owned company, I'd recommend reading *The Pirates of Manhattan* to put a finer point on the subject.[12] In short, at mutual companies, the life insurance contracts issued by the company are generally participating whole life contracts, meaning company profits are disbursed via dividends to the policyholders, not a separate class of misaligned-interest stockholders.

I arrived at the Los Angeles office with a fully developed PowerPoint presentation, presenting to the managing partner for over two hours all the challenges, opportunities, marketplace inefficiencies, and goals for my vision and business plan. By the end of our time together, the feeling was mutual (pun intended). We had struck an agreement that I would join her agency as a FINRA Series 24/Registered Principal to guide and develop the investment advisory work of more than two hundred branch-associated FINRA-registered representatives.

---

[12] Barry James Dyke, *The Pirates of Manhattan* (Portsmouth, NH: 555 Publishing, 2007).

The core of my proposal was rooted in the simple idea that serving clients in a commission-based transaction method was antiquated and inferior. Commission remuneration ends up being an expensive proposition for clients. Additionally, FAs bombard clients with the next greatest investment idea that just crossed their desk. Clients are not equipped to manage or evaluate the ideas presented. The client-broker interaction is a classic confidence relationship, defined by the quality of a familiar and comfortable interpersonal relationship developed over time. But it should also be defined by the knowledge that there's an evaluation on the quality of advice. Even though there are no assurances that the advice will yield desired results, there should at least be a process of evaluation.

Again, I had a great desire to highlight a suitability- versus a fiduciary-care standard because I'd like to believe financial advisors genuinely seek to hire the best money managers and properly monitor their replacement, but that's simply not my experience. Furthermore, the costs associated with changing managers (especially in pooled investment vehicles, but also applicable to separately managed accounts due to the cost of tax consequences) will eat into those desired returns due to up-front charges. More importantly, I believe that no one money-management institution could possibly be an effective or best-performing asset manager across all asset classes.

I witnessed my first employer having bought several money managers over the years, only to develop new packaged products to distribute, which then delivered lackluster investment results—but not lackluster business revenue for their distributors. With all the available published statistical research, money managers rarely (0.6 percent of the time, to be precise)[13] beat their assigned benchmark given one-, three-, five-, and ten-year time periods. I knew that there was a profound opportunity to show up in a different, more beneficial way in the advisor-client relationship.

Managed-money (also called separately managed accounts) platforms had been a core area of recommendation for this newly formed business plan. Managed money solves a few problems that transactional relationships create. Most every FA has access to these solutions currently, but since they do not pay as well, there's an underutilization.

Investors should be asking about the FA's access to such solutions. When doing so, make sure that there are no commissions or sales charges, but only a single all-inclusive fee. When thinking of managed money, I think of the analogy of the public transit bus versus a ride in a limo. The public bus is the mutual fund or pooled-investment product, where all the shareholders are subject to a uniform experience—whether it is performance, holdings, taxes, or volatility. Managed money is more like a limo ride, where the investor is not subject to a pooled experience, but a more individualized one. This allows for a more customized control of holdings, tax management, and even volatility, but not investment strategy.

Little did I know at that time that there was an even greater development yet to come; a diamond in the rough had been underutilized and formed as a wholly owned subsidiary

---

[13] Joe Light, "And the Next Star Fund Manager Is …," *Wall Street Journal*, January 17, 2014, http://www.wsj.com/articles/SB1000142405270230441 9104579324871451038920.

company at this mutual life insurance company only a couple of years prior to my joining in 2005.

I viewed the opportunity to change the advisor-client paradigm as my purpose, fighting the prevailing conflicted advice and resulting transactions that plague the retail investing public. I would articulate this perspective with a small army of insurance professionals who happened to also hold FINRA licenses. Sharing my stories of what really transpires in the Wall Street financial product development and distribution mechanisms might just find a following there.

More importantly, I sought to compete against the established brokerage houses with a poorly understood but highly superior fiduciary standard of care offering. A true fiduciary standard of care means that *only* the investor's best interest is being served—and no other interest is even considered. But much like the health-care and legal communities, the financial-services industry possesses one of the most powerful lobbying groups in Washington, DC, one that sees to it that their bread continues to be buttered in the manner they've become accustomed to.

I also thought about how special an opportunity this was. I was a capital markets professional, someone who'd worked inside the nontransparent world of Wall Street. Now this experience could be utilized by many trusted insurance advisors for their clients' benefit, bringing them an evolved service. *But … would these insurance-focused advisors see the opportunity for their clients?* They were used to compensation that was commission-based. Such was the manner of remuneration in the insurance business—up-front commissions equaling anywhere from 12 percent to over 100 percent of a client's first-year insurance premium. *Would this group engage in a business model that would pay a small fraction of revenue?* The comparative break-even compensation of a managed-money sale versus the sale of a mutual fund would be upward of five or more years. This was a new business line, however, and I hoped there *would* be FAs willing to join the crusade.

There were pros and cons to this new venture, undoubtedly. Like any entrepreneur understands, there is great risk, but as long as a commensurate amount of reward exists, then it's a worthy venture. The risk to me was obvious: the possibility that no one would give my philosophy the time of day, and that no one would relate or see the value that could be brought to their clients' lives. But being an optimist and one who always follows his gut, I dived into the abyss. It wasn't until years later that the opportunity evolved into a unique industry-changing service model. In a later chapter, we'll discuss this resulting innovation in the form of the *independent, noncaptive corporate trustee advisor,* which has become a relevant and more valued standard for wealth care today.

CHAPTER THREE

A Review of the Players Involved

Now that you've seen the areas I've worked in in the financial-services industry and what I've learned, I hope you can also start to see how that industry doesn't always serve the investor in the way the investor may think. As I worked through the ideas of changing the industry service model, I began to realize that retail investors and financial advisors would benefit from understanding more about these ideas.

Retail investors trust financial advisors to manage their money and trust that their advisor has their best interest in mind. But beyond the moniker of "financial advisor," retail investors may not know about the various licensed functions and FA roles in investor services. This chapter defines some of those roles, and a subsequent chapter discusses broker-versus-advisor differences in greater detail.

First, a retail investor is someone who transacts buy/sell orders for stocks, bonds, mutual funds, ETFs, and hundreds of other investment products. Retail investors use any of the following:

- *Broker/dealers*: A person or company that trades securities for its own account or for its clients. Some are independent brokers; others don't use advisors at all, as in do-it-yourself (DIY) platforms. Other broker/dealers are subsidiaries of investment companies or commercial banks. When the institution trades for itself, it's a dealer. When it trades on behalf of a customer, it's a broker. These employ FINRA-registered representatives, who've passed FINRA-administered exams called Series 7 (for the ability to sell general securities) or Series 6 (to sell only investment-company products, like mutual funds or unit investment trusts). It's a great idea to verify the licensing and complaint disclosures of any potential financial advisor by visiting FINRA's broker-check site, found at http://brokercheck.finra.org/.

- *Wire-house broker/dealers*, also known as full-service brokers, provide financial services to investors seeking to trade securities and/or engage investment advisory services, but the commissions and fees are usually higher. Wire-house firms are among the most popular choice for broker/dealer firms for the retail investing public. There used to be many, many more wire-house firms, but the Big 4 are now Merrill Lynch, Morgan

Stanley, UBS, and Wells Fargo. Wire-house brokers got their name from the late 1800s because they leased dedicated telegraph lines to transmit financial data more quickly.

- *Regional broker/dealers* are those with less expansive branch office locations nationally, usually focused within a particular geography; Crowell Weedon and Wedbush Morgan are examples. They provide similar services to wire houses.

- *Discounters* such as TD Ameritrade, Schwab, or Fidelity round out the bunch. Discount brokers provide DIY services to trade, for a fee that's lower than a full-service broker, but they don't provide customized financial advice. There's a current movement underway, called the *robo-advisor*, that's seeking to bring a higher level of financial advice combined with a low fee. Though a good idea, it fails to accomplish one of the more valuable roles of using an *ideal* financial advisor— preventing the investor from making emotion-based decisions. But, unfortunately, as we'll discuss later, advisors rarely guide clients away from investing emotions but rather use these to their sales advantage.

- *Registered investment advisors (RIAs)* are quite different from the broker/dealer product distribution model. RIAs are more about being the product itself—a money manager. These are the entities that manufacture and distribute their investment strategies through many thousands of mutual funds and other pooled-investment vehicles, as well as separately managed accounts. The Securities and Exchange Commission defines RIAs as an individual or a firm that is registered with the SEC and in the business of giving advice about securities. They are paid by percentage of assets they manage, an hourly fee, a fixed fee, or a commission, if the advisor is also a broker/dealer.

- *Investment advisor representative (IAR)*: Under the employ of a RIA, this is an individual who gives advice on investing in securities such as stocks, bonds, mutual funds, or exchange-traded funds. An IAR discloses conflicts and earns income from fees, not commissions. These conflicts are enumerated in their Form ADV. This form can be found on the SEC website, or better yet, a hard copy is required to be provided to clients upon opening a new account.

- *Wholesaler*: Wholesalers market the products of their money-management and RIA employers to a wide variety of financial institutions. A national sales manager routinely manages many dozens, sometimes hundreds, of external and internal wholesalers scattered across the country. Managing director and vice president are common titles for external wholesalers who are based in the field with specific geographic coverage. Internal wholesalers are often located in a central location to provide ongoing broad-based coverage and communications with the various distribution channels. These channels are broken into several subsets, like those introduced here, including the largest broker/dealers within the wire house, regional, independent, and registered investment advisor (RIA) markets.

Wholesalers are a very special breed of salespeople. I have now come to know hundreds. They are an essential tool in the dissemination of the intelligence (or lack thereof) and perspective from the best and worst money managers in the financial industry—but who can tell the difference? Only hindsight validates.

Money-management companies make the greatest use of these individuals in the distribution of their companies' proprietary products. Here is where it gets problematic. Most investors don't realize that there's this entire industry sales force—comprised of many tens of thousands—that go around waving pom-poms and cheerleading for their companies' products to audiences that consist of financial advisors located at every bank and brokerage firm in every corner of every town across the entire United States.

These wholesalers take great pride in setting to memory talking points about how and why their firms' money-management products are superior to the next. Financial advisors hear dozens of stories a month from external and internal wholesaling staff alike. Financial advisors are bombarded and perhaps even shell-shocked. Sometimes they get so angry and frustrated, they lash out in wholesaler presentations, yelling, barking, or even throwing a bagel or two.

The financial advisors are burdened with their own

brokerage company's distribution agenda, which is in close partnership with the various money-management firms. But they also, in many instances, want to do the best thing for their clients. The sad reality is that the financial and psychological paradigm that exists between money managers and brokers, who sell their products, is so deeply engrained that lifting out of this rut is next to impossible.

The system has determined how wholesalers, advisors (and their brokerage firms), and money managers are to provide a mutually beneficial and profitable financial arrangement among themselves. However, at the very center of this arrangement is the retail client investor, who is the pawn in this high-stakes game.

CRONY CAPITALISM: CAPITAL ALLOCATION'S ENEMY

I wanted to touch upon the issue of crony capitalism in its more philosophical sense. Capitalism is the heart of any investment scheme, but understanding the problems created in crony capitalism can help an investor understand more about how money is earned and lost in this industry. There are underpinnings to this discourse that are of practical use to any investor. It's included here since most financial advisors, who are marketed to by wholesalers, don't give this subject much thought at all. But the inherent conflicts of interest present in the money manager-distribution channel-retail investor client love triangle mean that there are broad consequences to our overall economy due to the industry's collusion and nontransparency. It would be ideal to have true free-market capitalism indeed, but we are nowhere near resembling that kind of utopia in the majority aspect of our socioeconomic hierarchy.

My grandfather would quote, cite, and make required reading the texts of most Austrian School economic thinkers. My own economic philosophy finds a comfortable home in the writings of Von Mises and Hayek.

Crony capitalism is one of the more wealth-destructive forces in any economy. I suggest that crony capitalism is as contrary a force as any despotic dictatorship, oligarchy, or Communistic ideology. However, due to the inclusion of the word *capitalism*, many people confuse the association for something beneficial.[14]

What is crony capitalism? It's when there are significant amounts of government intervention (e.g., payoffs, backroom deals, etc.) or regulation (e.g., legislation, tariffs, etc.). This market interference results in an immediate countereffect of inefficiency expansion within the economy. Such expansion is good for very few and bad for many, which is a root identifier of any inefficient modality within an operating system—like our capital markets. In private-sector ventures, risks have commensurate rewards; the greed factor motivates participants to engage in the game. All participants use their skills and talents to get more than their fair share. Failure and success are allowed to meet one another often in the marketplace. Mark Cuban, the multifaceted entrepreneur, has

---

[14] Prof. Richard Ebeling, "Free Market Capitalism vs. Crony Capitalism," *EPICTimes*, July 14, 2014, http://www.epictimes.com/2014/07/free-market-capitalism-vs-crony-capitalism/.

nicely articulated his perspective on capital allocation,[15] even remarking that if you sit down at the stock trading terminal and don't see who the loser is in a transaction, it's probably you.

Capital is a resource best allocated to the areas of the most favorable risk-adjusted product, service, manufacturing, or distribution channel. When capital-allocation decisions are being impugned by cronyism or other selective favoritism, the resulting economic system will develop severe pockets of inefficiencies, which tend to reward failure.

During the 2008 crisis, the fact that specific financial institutions were bailed out by government while others failed is an economic abomination. Institutions saved with a government bailout were rewarded for their reckless and arrogant positions in certain capital instruments. This action meant that other market participants, engaged in more prudent capital-allocation activities, were literally robbed of the opportunity to heal the market of capital-allocation inefficiencies. Insurers, in particular, had avoided much of the financial damages brought on by the economic crisis.[16] This capital-market inefficiency was created by the failed allocation decisions. An otherwise successful market participant would extend healing action in the form of healthier balance sheets through buying the depreciated assets of failed institutions,

---

[15] "The Stock Market Is Still for Suckers and Why You Should Put Your Money in the Bank," The Mark Cuban Weblog, August 20, 2010, http://blogmaverick.com/2010/08/20/the-stock-market-is-still-for-suckers-and-why-you-should-put-your-money-in-the-bank/.

[16] Sebastian Schich, "Insurance Companies and the Financial Crisis," *OECD Journal: Financial Market Trends* 2009, no. 2 (October 2009), http://www.oecd.org/finance/financial-markets/44260382.pdf.

buying them at pennies on the dollar—instead of the government being the purchaser; the government should only be a buyer of last resort.[17]

By circumventing the rational, organized proceedings of bankruptcy courts, the US government stole from the investor-healthier 401(k) and other investment vehicles balances. Though possibly the injury would have been temporarily more severe, the market "patient" would have had a sterile, emergency-room operation, and the risk of infection would have been muted via the administration of antibiotics (e.g., bankruptcy filings and settlements).

Those healthier institutions did not have an opportunity to swoop in and buy some former rivals on the cheap, thus removing the market's ability to experience capital-reallocation decisions through managed failures. This had the ultimate effect of removing a more robust, sustainable recovery unburdened by the current US $2.8 trillion debt-financed (albeit cheap debt) recovery model, which after several years might finally be at an end.[18] A market system void of nonmarket participants is the best way to ensure healthy market cycles of bear- and bull-market opportunities across industries.

In the meantime there are regulations trapped in the

---

[17] Peter Coy, "Alexander Hamilton Was Even More Amazing Than You Thought," *Bloomberg Businessweek—Global Economics*, May 9, 2014, http://www.businessweek.com/articles/2014-05-09/alexander-hamilton-was-even-more-amazing-than-you-thought.

[18] Ann Saphir, "With the End of Fed's QE in Sight, U.S. Public Says 'Huh?'" Reuters, September 17, 2013, http://www.reuters.com/article/2013/09/17/us-usa-fed-poll-idUSBRE98G18K20130917.

legislature that intend to protect investors' interests better. The truth is that only market participants will be able to evolve the financial-services industry to a higher standard of care, not regulators. Allow competition to dictate the winners and losers of winning investor capital. The key is educating investors that a substantive difference exists in wealth-care standards and helping them understand the profit benefit in the hiring of a higher care standard.

CHAPTER FOUR

A Broker by Any Other Name Would Still Smell

Currently there is great interest in the regulatory world to better clarify for the investing public who is a broker (someone who trades) versus an advisor (someone who gives you advice based on your goals and not his or her commission). "Financial advisor" has become a generic term for many different types of roles, and retail investors may not easily see that there are different nuances to the different titles, so the advisor isn't as neutral as one would expect.

Does your FA serve in a true advisory role? Is he or she compensated based on your success or failure due to the advice he or she disseminates or just on the dissemination of the product? In the real estate industry, there is no confusion on the conflicts around realtors, who serve as real estate brokers, earning commissions from the transacting of real estate. A seller's price reduction might mean a swifter sale but result in many tens of thousands of dollars less in proceeds, whereas the realtor only suffers perhaps several hundreds of dollars lost.

However, there is a gray fog around when a client is working with his or her financial advisor, who is a FINRA Series 65 or 66, which allows the advisor to function as an IAR or investment advisor representative. FINRA regulates financial representatives, giving examinations (series) for the various levels. A registered representative (RR) or broker (also regularly called a financial advisor) must pass a Series 7 and 63 examination; an IAR must pass just a Series 66 (or combo Series 63 + 65) examination. Most often, especially at wire houses, FAs have both capabilities. Where do the regulations overlap, and when is the client properly notified? FINRA is governing that registered representative, as is the SEC, providing the IAR with the beginnings of a fiduciary standard of care. The FINRA-only registered broker (a FINRA Series 6 or 7 RR or registered representative) is subject to very distinct regulations and lower-care standards. The investing public doesn't know, and the potential for conflicts of interest in investing the client's money abounds.

I think it wholly unsatisfactory and insulting to the investing public that there's not a more transparent delineation between IAR and RR because both are called financial advisors. In providing clarity, the financial-advisory industry would better serve the client's understanding of the standard of care the client is engaging and trusting. Additionally, every commission-remunerated product sale, along with other securities and nonpooled investments, should be disclosed in a special, separate client-signed form explaining the precise amount of revenues, both hard and soft dollars, generated to the broker/dealer entity, as well as the individual RR.

Accordingly, the industry should not let corporate registered investment advisors (CRIAs, also referred to as just financial advisors) disguise their conflicts of interests, either. Most are intimately engaged in complicated marketing partnership remuneration agreements. IAs and CRIAs are required to file annually their Form ADV with the SEC. The form has two parts. Part 1 requires information about the business and is a series of check boxes. According to the SEC, Part 2 requires investment advisors to prepare narrative brochures written in plain English that contain information such as the types of advisory services offered, the advisor's fee schedule, disciplinary information, conflicts of interest, and the educational and business background of management and key advisory personnel of the advisor.

These filings are available to the public on the IAPD (Investment Adviser Public Disclosure) website. If most investors took the time to read the corporate or even independent RIA's ADV Part 2 filings with the SEC, they would run, not walk, in the opposite direction.

Form ADVs are drafted in quasi-legalese, making them difficult to understand, even though the SEC regulation makes it clear that they should be in plain English. These forms literally have entire chapters with titles like "Conflicts of Interests" (COIs), where in no uncertain terms, clients can read all the myriad ways in which their investment is helping to support other institutional agendas and revenues.

As a former employee for one of the largest RIA money managers on Wall Street (my first employer had many capabilities), I've seen how this occult dynamic is very lucrative for distribution channels and money managers alike. Having COIs is certainly not illegal, or even considered unethical by the SEC, because it is compliant with an SEC fiduciary standard of care to *disclose conflicts*. By no means would I believe that a client is being served in a *true* fiduciary capacity simply because a company discloses a conflict. A true fiduciary puts only the client's interests at the core of the service engaged, and no other interest can play a role.

Typically, the Form ADV is provided (or should be) alongside any proposal from an RIA or IAR. Make it a special point to ask your advisor to pull out his or her personal and the company's Form ADV Parts 1 and 2. Then, have the advisor walk you through the various chapters. These chapters are revealing in the areas of total fees and expenses charged, as well as conflicts of interest. If the advisor has hesitation in producing or reviewing these items, it's best to cross him or her off your list and move on to the next advisor.

The most interesting aspect of my institutional career was the advisor (either FA or RR or IAR) conversations. These advisors (who were my clients at the time) working at various brokerage houses were always encouraged and pressured into listening to our product *de jour* pitches, as it was another path toward meeting sales quotas for the month. I'm very glad to admit this, but not every broker was like this or engaged for such self-preservation and interest.

There are some great FAs who actually evolved into IARs

and chose to only serve clients in a percentage-of-assets fee compensation. Of course, as discussed previously, this still posed recommendation conflicts due to the institutional distributor revenue-sharing partnerships with money-management firms. But this was an incremental step in a more evolved direction.

I witnessed very, very few (less than a half dozen out of five thousand FAs) that were not motivated by and were disinterested in the financial remuneration from both product distribution commissions and other forms of remuneration (e.g., "marketing support dollars"—paid both at the firm-wide level and the individual-rep level). These support dollars essentially created a partnership interest between the money-manager firm and the distributing broker, thereby eliminating an objective, conflict-free recommendation environment. These exceptional few financial advisors were a true aberration from the norm. It was inspiring.

A financial advisor's duplicity is in serving two masters—the hired money manager and his or her retail investor client—and is therefore incongruous with truly objective advice. No one can serve two masters in equally effective, unbiased procedures. Think of various invitations that you may have received from advisors to attend a dinner or luncheon for an education seminar, or perhaps, a client-appreciation event with a guest speaker of some repute. The sponsoring mutual fund or money manager, or other financial product manufacturers, typically pay the costs wholly or substantially for these events. In exchange for this support, these companies expect a return on their investment, meaning receiving asset flows in the form of product sales from the supported advisor. *How could this be in the client's best interest?*

The answer is, of course, that it's not. Learn more about your financial advisor's true functional capacity—review his or her FINRA broker check and read Form ADV. The next chapters talk about the regulations and then how you can audit your advisor in order to keep or fire him or her.

CHAPTER FIVE

Legislated vs. Self-Regulated Authorities and Oversight

The entire product manufacturing and distribution process is regulated by the SEC and FINRA. This regulation does not prevent a significant shadow remuneration element (hidden compensation or fees), which is poorly disclosed to clients and, certainly even worse, unquestioned by the investing public. How does one know how to ask details on something that he or she doesn't even know exists? It's akin to the recent phenomenon of a black swan event—you don't know it exists and therefore can't identify it until you see it.

FINRA

FINRA is the Financial Industry Regulatory Authority, and we noted in the previous chapter how FINRA designates different classes of investment advisors. It is a self-regulating agency, a not-for-profit agency authorized by Congress to ensure the securities industry operates fairly and honestly. Unfortunately, it falls short of this goal.

At FINRA there are roughly three thousand employees who are involved in the policing, monitoring, and surveillance of the 635,000 broker/dealer RRs and tens of thousands of broker/dealer firms. The most interesting aspect about all this work is that reviewing the vast number and subject of complaints (formally filed with the regulator in writing) against these member firms is quite revealing to the core problem of financial product distribution. FINRA proudly boasts 1,535 disciplinary actions against RRs just in 2013 and more than $60 million in levied fines.[19] What if FINRA's fine revenue decreased? It would be a good thing for investors, but not something that FINRA would be happy about, since it would lead to layoffs, which would in turn reduce its ability to police and run audit campaigns. There's a natural incentive to keep the fine revenue stable or growing, which is a conflict of another ilk.

The suitability standard of care—the bar, if you will—is set so low that, frankly, the retail investing public is unaware. The standard of care that is set forth means that the RR is held harmless (though not beyond reproach) as long as he or she has collected a thorough understanding that provides a justifiable and relevant rationale as to why at the *time* of the product recommendation, it was in fact suitable to the goals, needs, objectives, and risk tolerance of the investor.

To many investors this may come as somewhat of a shock.

---

[19] *FINRA 2013 Year in Review and Annual Financial Report*, FINRA, 2014, https://www.finra.org/file/finra-2013-year-review-and-annual-financial-report.

Many investors have come to understand, as it is in fact marketed to them, that they are dealing with a financial advisor, so they expect *advice*. The two terms *advisor* and *broker* are not synonymous. An advisor provides advice and is compensated on an ongoing basis related to the quality of the advice. A broker is compensated based on the sale of a recommended product based on the time of the recommendation. These are completely different jobs with completely separate alignment of interests between advisor and client versus broker and client.

The problem in today's investment-services world is that this difference is poorly disclosed and little, if any, education is done by the industry or the media. Why would either the industry or the media want to cut from under the industry the very bulk core of its revenue streams (commissions), which would in turn then cut the funding to advertising campaigns from which big media rake their profits? There's just no universal standard of what to call our various types of financial advisors.

There are many professionals and fringe legislators who argue, as do I, that the term *advisor* should only be used by those reps who do not engage in product sales compensated by commissions. But how does that work in reality? An investor meets a registered representative (RR) at a friend's cocktail party, they exchange cards, and the RR's card reads "Financial Advisor." After they meet and discuss and chat some more, the distinction between what is "advice" versus introducing a product that is being "brokered" or sold is forever lost into the ether. The investor has a presumption of a certain level of wealth care that does not in fact exist. The standard of care is so very low with suitability when measured against the investor's time frame of evaluation. This example is useful since the financial advisor may have also had access to separately managed accounts or other fee-based services but chose instead to "ring the cash register" through product sales for this particular client. *How does the client get to understand the FA's rationale as to why one service model is better for him or her than another?*

The sheer volume of complaints against firms and RRs and the resulting millions in FINRA restitution settlements and penalties[20] reveals a fundamental flaw in the investor's understanding of the quality and motivation of the recommendations versus having an experience of true advice in the investor's best interest.

SEC

The Securities Exchange Commission (SEC), unlike FINRA, is a regulator legislated into existence after the stock-market crash of 1929. According to investor.gov, its mission is to protect investors; maintain fair, orderly, and efficient markets; and facilitate capital formation. Its responsibilities are manifold. The SEC registers new-issue securities, like IPOs, for both investment companies (e.g., closed-end funds, etc.) and traditional capital raising for operating companies (e.g., IBM, Walmart, etc.). There was a time when the vast

---

[20] Liz Skinner, "FINRA Reports Dramatic Jump in Restitution in 2012," *Investment News*, January 8, 2013, http://www.investmentnews.com/article/20130108/ FREE/130109952/finra-reports-dramatic-jump-in-restitution-in-2012.

majority of capital-raising activity was for the benefit of a real business enterprise, unlike now, where many billions more are raised for pooled investment vehicles that buy other financial products.

Also, the SEC oversees the registered investment advisor marketplace (and the products they issue, like mutual funds, unit investment trusts, exchange-traded funds, closed-end funds, and so on). There's a threshold that sets a $25 million mandate of registration, below which RIAs do not have to be federally regulated.

The confusing part of this is that both FINRA and the SEC issue regulations for financial professionals. The investing public does not have the sophistication to discern between a financial professional who is regulated by the SEC, FINRA, or neither, and the business cards of all these "financial professionals" use similar names. Even with FINRA and SEC regulations, there is no way to force the separation of an advisor from broker activities. Adding insult to injury is the fact that those non-FINRA or SEC-licensed professionals who solely engage in the sale of life insurance or other insurance-based products (like fixed and indexed annuities) have monikers like "Financial Professional" or "Financial Consultant" on their business cards.

DODD-FRANK ACT

Congress also plays an active role in regulation in that it can pass laws that govern securities. A brokered sale of securities by a FINRA-registered representative is subject to a *suitability* standard of care, called a "suitable sale." This standard of care currently is under hot debate via the Wall Street Reform and Consumer Protection Act, a.k.a. the Dodd-Frank Act, signed into law on July 21, 2010. The Act has been trying, thus far unsuccessfully, to redefine the suitability rule that registered reps are subject to. Over $1 billion has been spent by the financial-services industry in steering away from the bill's intended efficacy.[21]

In my opinion Dodd-Frank will be partially repealed— especially in the areas that discuss *suitability* versus *fiduciary*, specifically the new proposed fiduciary standard for registered reps, which is still being debated even after the SEC's study on the subject was released on January 21, 2011.[22] Again, the suitability standard of care means as long as the recommendation was appropriate to the investor based on his or her overall goals, financial objectives, overall risk tolerance, and time horizon *at the time of the sale*, the broker has done an adequate job of making an appropriate recommendation. *How could this have ever been an accepted standard?* No investor buys investments thinking how relevant they are to his or her *current* state of goals and objectives. People buy an investment for how it *will serve future* goals and objectives.

---

[21] Gary Rivlin, "How Wall Street Defanged Dodd-Frank," *Nation*, May 20, 2013. Gary Rivlin is an Investigative Fund reporting fellow at the Nation Institute, http://www.thenation.com/article/174113/how-wall-street-defanged-dodd-frank.

[22] Barry R. Temkin and Michael R. Koblenz, "New Suitability and Fiduciary Standards for Financial Advisers Under the Wall Street Reform Act and FINRA Rules," *Securities Arbitration Commentator* 2010, no. 2 (March 2011), http://www.moundcotton.com/sites/default/files/NewSuitabilityAndFiduciaryStandards.pdf.

Why would the purveyor of an investment not have the similar and aligned duty and compensation time frame for his or her recommendations?

Sadly, *suitability* is a flawed invention of the industry that stacks the deck against the investor from day one. The reality is that almost every investor wants substantially the same outcome when it comes to his or her investments. Everyone would like to make as much money as possible in the bull markets and lose as little money as possible in the bear markets. Or, said another way, make as much money as they can with as little risk to the capital as possible.

This is, in fact, the Holy Grail of modern portfolio theory, which few are ever likely to achieve.

There is one more regulator. It is the only financial regulator that is an actual division of the US government (the Department of the Treasury), not just a commission legislated into existence (e.g., the SEC) or a self-regulatory organization (SRO) like FINRA. I've shared this fact to professional audiences across the United States, and not once has a professional "financial advisor" understood these differences.

CHAPTER SIX

FINRA, SEC, and OCC ... Wait, Who?

When I Google "OCC" from my home in California, I get results for Orange Coast College and Orange County Choppers—and only at the bottom of the page a reference to the one I'm highlighting here. That's how under the radar this authority operates. The OCC (or Office of the Comptroller of the Currency) successfully merged with the OTS (Office of Thrift Supervision) in 2010.

The OCC is the *only* US financial industry regulator, whose supervised banks specifically take on fiduciary duties to serve clients with the client's "best and only interest" as the sole directive for a foundation of such interaction with clients. These banks can even be nonlending institutions, which therefore removes yet another layer of risk taking from their operations. The OCC is not an entity that is well-known or understood, but it is the only federal regulator that is an actual component of the US government, as it is embedded within the US Department of the Treasury. It is similar to the FDIC but far savvier to the world of investment and asset management, and not solely bound to dealing with capitalization and reserve concerns.

An OCC-regulated entity is subject to very high scrutiny and rigorous operational audits. Regardless of our opinions on government operations, wouldn't any investor feel better and prefer having the federal government come in and conduct a six-week audit of all his or her accounts on a regular cycle of eighteen months? This is what you'll get with an OCC audit schedule. Think of how upset people are when they learn they'll be audited by the Internal Revenue Service, and this will give you a sense of the scrutiny of the OCC, but with regular frequency and vigor. Compare this to the irregular, sporadic audits from FINRA and the SEC.

The reason I believe there's an importance to who regulates and audits the activities of the financial-services firm is because I've seen firsthand the impact on clients during times of crisis. All three entities—FINRA, SEC, and the OCC—have roughly the same number of employees: three thousand. But as mentioned before, FINRA and the SEC have many hundreds of thousands of individuals and many tens of thousands of business entities to manage.

The OCC has only about two thousand entities to manage and therefore doesn't have to pick its surveillance agenda the way FINRA and the SEC must. FINRA must choose certain regulatory themes year-to-year, messaged to their broker/dealer network. One year they may care more about a certain sales practice, and yet another year, a product concern. None of these is specific to any individual's experience, as it's more akin to the bus analogy provided in an earlier chapter.

The SEC is not much different, as it too must be reactive and rely on whistle-blowers for where to point its attention. But as we learned with the Madoff scheme, even a persistent whistle-blower, as in that case, does not mean a speedy regulatory intervention.[23]

The sad reality is that good financial professionals are taken on misrepresented and poorly understood risky investment journeys quite frequently and not necessarily by Ponzi schemes. For example, take the debacle of Dutch market auctions and preferred-rate securities. Many brokers improperly used such preferred-rate securities as cash equivalents, having for many decades utilized this security type as a cash equivalent, often providing a better yield than bank savings or a money-market account. There had never been an instance where liquidity was a concern, as these had been regularly liquidated in an effective marketplace through a Dutch auction process.

It wasn't until 2008 that suddenly the market had changed. Owners of these securities thought they had been invested in a cash-equivalent security with great liquidity, but these securities were now inconveniently *frozen*. Clients invested

---

[23] Allan Chernoff, Sr. Correspondent, CNN, "*Madoff Whistleblower Blasts SEC,*" February 4, 2009. This report includes the following quote: "A fraud investigator told Congress that he'd warned the agency about Madoff's Ponzi scheme years ago. But his efforts went nowhere." http://money.cnn.com/2009/02/04/news/newsmakers/madoff_whistleblower/.

in auction-rate preferreds, as they are also called, were unable to use these funds—many of which had been used as a parking place as they awaited escrow deals to close and the like. Many months passed before slowly the spigot began to allow for flow again, and some are still waiting years later.[24] Meanwhile, many lawsuits also mounted against the sponsors and distributors of these products. But ultimately, the advisors who used these products, who were aware of the risks—but not sophisticated enough—are to blame, as were the broker/dealer firms that did not do enough to educate their advisors.

Many financial professionals tell great stories to their clients, thus illustrating the basic issue: that if any investment program pays a broker a commission, there is a serious conflict of interest. This type of remuneration will be a relic in years to come, but only because clients choose to custody their monies away from such conflicts and the companies that purport those behaviors. In this prior example, what if these brokers were paid based on access to funds and penalized for loss of liquidity? Perhaps then there would have been more attention paid to the product sponsor's fine print.

Recently I spoke with a successful investment advisor representative (IAR), who was truly surprised and shocked to learn about the differences in the standards of care among regulators. His argument started out as "all the investment platforms out there are the same." Only after I itemized some of the aforementioned significant regulatory differences

---

[24] Daisy Maxey, "For Many Auction-Rate Investors, the Freeze Goes On," *Wall Street Journal*, March 13, 2012, http://www.wsj.com/articles/SB100014240 52970203960804577243554110930094.

among FINRA, the SEC, and the OCC did his argument begin to wilt. Most good financial advisors do have their clients' interests at heart, but what I am challenging is whether a financial advisor has *only* his or her clients' interests at heart. No advisor should have an alternate source of income other than the agreed compensation that comes from the client. More ideally, compensation should *only* be based upon a client's account's month-end market value. Such an advisor would have a far more vested interest in the value of a client's account.

However, the reality is that financial advisors have so many conflicted interests that the question has become whether those amount to something critical or superficial. Either way, wouldn't everyone agree we would want to reduce conflicts as much as possible, if not eliminate them altogether?

The notion that clients believe that their financial advisors have to make a living and understand there will be costs associated with doing business is a rational belief. However, this is impugned by the circumstances around the advisor that burdens or guides his or her behavior in a manner that does not have as a sole priority the client's best interest.

Furthermore, in my prior career working on the institutional asset-management distribution, I worked down the hall from the founding team of the largest independent RIA platforms in the United States. Back then we clearly understood the great work being done on an asset-based fee compensation basis versus the commission-based brokerage industry. But there are still conflicts between the fee-based platform and the money managers who populate them.

Money-management companies employ personnel called key account managers to develop profitable partnership relationships with distribution channels using all legal, but not necessarily ethical, means available.

What I'm suggesting is that not enough is being done along the continuum of eliminating conflicts within asset-based fee-dispensed advice, even though I readily agree that this is better than brokers who are commission-based.

I think an OCC entity is doing a better job addressing these issues. However, it's still up to each entity to go further than prescribed regulation to truly root out conflicts. For example, many OCC firms use their own proprietary mutual funds or money managers to populate their client portfolios. I've even witnessed how some OCC-regulated firms will provide more favorable credit lines on proprietary assets versus nonproprietary assets. Advisors and clients alike must remain ever vigilant against the corporate proprietary agenda. Doing so will better safeguard a client's portfolio against conflicts of interest that may hurt performance, increase tax bills (due to forced liquidation of proprietary funds that can't transfer to other platforms), and increase expenses.

Wall Street is the one street that profits from both failures and successful investments, whereas Main Street simply profits from only successful ones. This simple truth lies in the fact that Wall Street is not only on both sides of the transaction but also the facilitator of it, whereas the retail investor is simply the consumer of institutional products and agendas. Some retail investors might profit from time to time, but all institutional players, whether a product manufacturer or distributor, profit from distribution and underwriting fees regardless of the investment's performance.

This will continue to be the paradigm until the industry is pressured to change through investor demand. This change will most likely be led by companies that are operating with honorable, sustainable, trustworthy, credible methods. Business media should champion these methods, bringing special attention to alternate advisory platforms in the financial-industry marketplace. The only way we can witness an evolution is for the industry to transform from within, to become a better-adapted version of itself, after acknowledging its inability to thrive long-term in its current state. The financial-services industry has yet to come to this realization. Only when its profits are affected will there be a deep desire to evolve to better suit the consumer's demand for a higher standard of wealth care.

A New System of Disclosure?

Ethics is the most client-valued component to business operations and decision making. If business fosters a transparent and open-architecture agenda, then in fact those businesses contribute productively to their economies.

The disproportionate information and data sets between purveyors and consumers reveal the intrinsic opportunity for the consumer to lose in any and all transactions, where only one party, the purveyor, always benefits. Maybe this is why so many people treat the stock market like a casino,[25] since everyone knows deep down that the house always wins.

The financial system today is at its height of dysfunction and inefficiency as measured by the volume of data afforded to

---

[25] Justin Lahart, "Maybe This Is Why the Stock Market Gets Called a Casino ...," *Wall Street Journal*, November 4, 2013, http://blogs.wsj.com/economics/2013/11/04/maybe-this-is-why-the-stock-market-gets-called-a-casino/.

the general public for dissemination and consumption. There is so much data available, more than at any time in history, and yet bear markets occur with additional volatility. New disasters are manifest, like flash crashes and IPO failures, along with old favorites like people still losing all their investment dollars on an idea that they discovered through a newsletter, business TV program, or newspaper. It should be a crime to disseminate any financial product information to the general public in such a manner, but it's very much allowed since these publishers are exempt from oversight.[26] Rules governing financial products are actually most like those of gambling, mainly *caveat emptor* or "let the buyer beware." In reality speculation is the bulk of retail investing activity.

THE SPECULATION ADVISOR

To the below-average investor, investing *is* gambling—but without the free drinks. Speculating is equivalent to gambling and should be properly termed with retail investing consumers. FINRA-regulated firms should consider the term "speculation advisor," not "financial advisor," for their registered reps who work as transactional, commissioned-based brokers. *Financial advisor* should only be considered a term to be used by verified conflict-free fiduciary asset and liability managers or advisors. Using the moniker of *speculation advisor* will clearly denote to prospective clients of a would-be "gambler with your money"

---

[26] Section 202(a)(11)(D) of the Investment Advisors Act of 1940, As Amended Through P.L. 112-90, Approved January 3, 2012, https://www.sec.gov. about/laws/iaa40.pdf.

that this particular relationship is potentially fraught with peril, and thus only proceed at your very deliberate discretion.

Speculation advisors would be free of fiduciary standards, free to earn commissions armed with their lowly level of a suitability-care standard. It could be that some speculation advisors would also be licensed to serve as financial advisors (under SEC rules), but if such a capacity were present—in any way to the client—it would have to be disclosed to the client, and the client would have to authorize through signature any speculation-advisor trade (e.g., one resulting in a commissionable event).

The state of New York is already engaged in an argument within the insurance industry that all sales documents must be accompanied by a full disclosure of all commissions paid by the insurance carrier to the selling agent or representative (currently Regulation 194 states that such information is provided upon request[27]). It is a brilliant concept that has little chance of getting passed in any legislature, since the insurance lobby has a strong and hefty PAC operating at both state and federal levels. This would also impact annuities (fixed, income, deferred, variable, and so on) that are sold by many non-FINRA registered "financial professionals," not to be confused with "financial advisors," not to be confused with our new term "speculation advisors."

Full disclosure is not the enemy of the financial-services industry, but a fundamental element of evolving accountability and responsibility from the financial-advisory sector. We are

---

[27] Regulation 194—Frequently Asked Questions—11 NYCRR 30 (Regulation 194), http://www.dfs.ny.gov/insurance/faqs/faqs-reg194.htm.

entering a critical time in the history of the financial world, where the largest and most productive population (by measure of created wealth measured in trillions) will be retiring continually for another fourteen years. This baby-boomer population needs our care and duty, especially since research estimates that 75 percent of Americans nearing retirement in 2010 had less than $30,000 in their retirement accounts.[28] Every financial firm should begin freely electing to disclose commissions without the burden of regulators.

Imagine if this level of transparency existed today—where a customer who is considering the purchase of a financial product through a broker would have all details of remuneration disclosed on a separate document for client signature, not buried twenty pages into a securities prospectus written by attorneys charged with "full disclosure," which amounts to unintelligible prose.

There are a multitude of scenarios, client needs, goals, and objectives where any specific financial product is completely relevant and, in fact, necessary given the client's unique situation to achieve the client's objectives. But letting clients know all the compensation, both hard *and* soft dollars, a product manufacturer will pay to the selling representative and his or her firm is a helpful fact, material to the transaction.

As mentioned previously on real estate, a broker's commission is itemized very clearly in closing documents.

---

[28] Edward Siedle, Contributor, "The Greatest Retirement Crisis in American History," Forbes.com, March 20, 2013, http://www.forbes.com/sites/edwardsiedle/2013/03/20/the-greatest-retirement-crisis-in-american-history/.

It doesn't mean real estate investors run screaming from the table when they see 6 percent in broker's commissions; rather, participants sign documents understanding better what is going on and which players are more motivated to see this transaction take place.

The day will come when every commission dollar and expected other affiliated revenue line from a financial product sale will appear as a matter of record, with signed client acknowledgment. I believe that the disclosures will include more detail than simply the monies earned from that specific transaction or account opening, but also include ancillary and related soft-dollar supports. These soft dollars can be at the broker/dealer level (divided into a "per rep" assignment) or can be specific marketing dollars a rep will receive from a particular product vendor for any number of marketing initiatives.

This type of *"Financial Professional or Registered Representative Transaction Benefit Statement"* might look something like this:

Dear Client:

You are engaging in this transaction ... The financial representative will make or is promised the following revenues on this transaction.

Commissions from product sponsor/ vendor ... 7%

> Anticipated marketing support dollars from
> vendor ... $5,000
> Additional bonus from hitting company
> thresholds ... $10,000
> Increased grid payout due to reaching next
> level ... $15,000
> Special recognition ... plaques, conference
> invitations, allowances

With advances in technology, itemizing the possible and planned remuneration sources for each client prior to transaction execution will not only be possible, but truly necessary. Disclosure is the means to prevent further abuse of the financial product distribution system, where investors end up buying things they don't really need and can't tell the difference. This type of disclosure will be the new standard, driven into existence through baby-boom investor demand so they may prevent retirement savings destruction. Ask for and read ADV forms.

REVEALING AN ADVISOR'S SOURCE OF INCOME

In addition to the *Financial Professional or Registered Representative Transaction Benefit Statement* illustrated, we could engage in a new universal system of disclosure, one that at its core has a standard poster of lettering or abbreviations that easily conveys the standard of care, liability, and regulation offered, as well as perhaps conveys to the public the source of income to the advisor.

Here are two examples of how the financial-services industry could be more descriptive in the capabilities and wealth care that a financial-services professional is subject to:

- The work of an advisor who functions as a fiduciary (abbr. *"Fid."*) and defined as a financial professional with more than 80 percent of compensation gained from advisory fees. Ideally there would be an independent audit that no remuneration or support dollars were received for the RR's benefit of client acquisition or retention from any product manufacturer (e.g., investment companies, insurance companies).
- Another classification could be listed as "broker sans conflict" (abbr. *"Brk.s.con"*), defined as an RR who earns commissions but does not take any funds or support from product vendors or sponsors, including trips or other perks.

These are examples of how much room for improvement there is, but also how convoluted it would be. Moving toward a universal standard, however, would help clarify the variety of duty to which advisors are beholden. However, there's little hope that FINRA could positively impact the current investment distribution practices that churn out sales based on transaction fees and conflicts of interest between distributors and money managers. Even under SEC scrutiny, it's certainly no better. These organizations are barely keeping up with their current workload. How could they embark on such an industry overhaul?

There are so many RIA shops that are not even federally registered, but only state-registered. This is ridiculous since such an arbitrary number (whether $25 million or $50 million assets under management thresholds) gives little solace to the retirees who put their $250,000 IRA rollover money with a nonfederally regulated entity (due to smaller size) that they were referred to by friends, only to discover that after years of money on deposit, that entity was a Ponzi scheme or worse. Unfortunately, even if the SEC is actively regulating such a RIA entity, the opportunity for significant supervisory failure still exists, *a la* Madoff. Since Madoff's scheme there have been over five hundred more uncovered, totaling more than $50 billion.[29] I suspect there are many schemes today that have yet to be revealed.

Seeing that Madoff was one of the most respected persons under FINRA and SEC jurisdictions, why would anyone trust these regulatory institutions at all? The definition of insanity is doing the same thing over and over and expecting a different result or outcome. So, why would any investor trust the system of regulation when it so clearly has failed in monumental proportion?

---

[29] Jordan Maglich, Contributor, "A Ponzi Pandemic: 500+ Ponzi Schemes Totaling $50Billion in 'Madoff Era,'" *Forbes Magazine*, February 12, 2014, http://www.forbes.com/sites/jordanmaglich/2014/02/12/a-ponzi-pandemic-500-ponzi-schemes-totaling-50-billion-in-madoff-era/.

CHAPTER EIGHT

Find a Corporate Trustee Advisor

Recently I received an invitation from an associate director of development from my alma mater to have lunch on her next trip to New York. There's been an excitement for the past few years to engage in this conversation. Our household has discussed as part of our legacy planning, establishing a scholarship for financial aid. I benefited from such scholarship funds and believe it imperative to give back in the same manner. The reason I bring this up is that this kind of philanthropic planning, which can be bundled into legacy planning, is best stewarded by an entity that is not limited to life expectancy.

Any kind of estate planning that is considering the distribution or disposition of assets beyond the current holder's life should give serious consideration to the use of a special kind of trustee relationship, called an institutional or corporate trustee. Families with a total net worth of at least

$10 million, or much less even depending on family dynamic and issues, should have a family trust or living trust drafted by an experienced trust and estate attorney.

I was meeting one such trust and estate attorney at her house in Long Island for Sunday brunch. She is like-minded in family wealth stewardship, in that to be done properly involves a team of fiduciary-based advisors. She made the very astute observation that what I talk about with all this "sense of duty" and "family fiduciary-based service" is akin to turning back the clock to a time when the family banker was an integral part of the family. This old-timey throwback professional joined in at the family birthday parties, celebrations, and BBQs, and typically maintained those relations throughout the lives of the patriarchs and matriarchs into the next generation until they retired with a gold watch, only to continue the intimacy and closeness as an "advisory board" member to the new generation. This was a time when there was less personnel turnover and advisors remained lifelong companions to their client families.

This concept is the founding element of evolving the financial world from a culture of proprietary corporate interest into truly guiding clients to their best interest, making recommendations and decisions that are in the client's sole interest, even if it means away from the proprietary agenda. And in our current financial zeitgeist, everyone should be seeking a more conflict-free service.

Corporate trustee entities, especially those audited and regulated by the OCC, are the best institutions suited to fulfill the role of intergenerational steward and serve as institutional or corporate trustees to the family's governing documents. These entities will combine the ongoing oversight of the family's assets, as well as investment management services that are in accordance with the parameters dictated in the family's governing documents or investment policy statement.[30] An investment policy statement (IPS) is an organizing document that governs the mandate of investments held within a trust account. It spells out how much of which asset class can be owned at any moment in time, as well as many other aspects. Rarely do FAs use IPS documents for their client accounts, but they are needed frequently.

For most of this book, I have discussed the variety of ways in which individual investors are at the mercy of (or more simply, pawns in) an institutional, proprietary agenda. This basic argument has significant impact, particularly in the areas of estate planning. Typically in estate planning, family members or close friends are asked to serve as trustees for family trusts once a triggering event like incapacitation or death occurs. The resulting execution of the trust documents does not usually resemble anything like the intention of the original grantor.

Simply put, individual trustees are human beings with emotions. Numerous studies conducted by behavioral finance researchers from around the country concur on the

---

[30] Thomas Forrest, CPA, AEP, "How a Corporate Trustee Can Help a Financial Planner Meet Their Client's Goals," *Journal of Financial Service Professionals* 61, no. 6 (November, 2007), https://www.naepc.org/journal/issue06g.pdf.

emotion-driven decision-making process that haunts every investor.[31] Primal instincts, coupled with herd mentality, are a sad and very financially destructive force. As a matter of opinion, I proffer that it is the emotion-based decision-making process of evaluation of investment buying or selling that presents one of the greatest threats to wealth preservation of families, more than any other source.

This is a slant against the mainstream media's preoccupation with screaming out, "Buy, buy, buy" or "Sell, sell, sell." There is no benefit to business media television (or Internet trading service tools) to educate investors, since their revenues are derived from the facilitators of chaos or those with proprietary, conflicted agendas.[32] It is merely preying upon the natural laws of human fight (greed) or flight (fear) instincts—survival of the fittest wrapped around a societal invention of wealth accumulation.

In the decades prior to technology, mostly institutional professionals were the primary investors in companies, after appropriate due diligence and rational research had been conducted on an investment opportunity. In the advent of democratic access to financial data, the boom of 401(k) participation, and readily sold financial products is

---

[31] For a variety of studies on the subject of behavioral finance, Yale School of Management and the International Center for Finance have an excellent resource center, found at http://som.yale.edu/faculty-research/our-centers/international-center-finance/research-initiatives/behavioral-finance.

[32] Madeline Vann, MPH, "Managing Stress in Tough Economic Times," Medically reviewed by Cynthia Haines, MD, *Everyday Health*, December 22, 2009, http://www.everydayhealth.com/emotional-health/managing-stress-in-bad-economy.aspx.

an assumption that such evolution is useful and beneficial to those who consume it. The proliferation of investment data and research is akin to a medical reference website; however, WebMD.com and other medical advice websites do not bombard their readers/viewers with do-it-yourself home operation kits. The thought is absurd. Financial health is treated by a professional standard of care that is completely out of alignment with the Hippocratic corpus ("first, do no harm") that the medical community strives toward (not without its own unique challenges, of course). At least folk aren't performing self-surgery at home.

These same emotions yield generally poor decision making around investments due to fear and greed, as mentioned before, and are the major derailment factors in a family's wealth-transfer agenda. Also, refer back to chapter 2 with research citations on the challenges of having money last beyond the second generation due to lack of communication. Generally I see three main areas of concern around appointing individuals as a *sole* trustee in a family's governing documents.

1) Individuals are *not audited by an independent regulatory authority.* There is peril for families who may appoint someone they trust or believe to be highly competent. I have seen all too often how a trusted friend or family member transforms into a dictator or, worse, someone who succumbs to predatory sales tactics or predatory friends and family who take advantage of the individual's lack of experience in prudent asset management. This lack of experience and little understanding of the assumed

liabilities of being a trustee are very real-world weaknesses. For example, a trustee's duty to inform and to account for trust activities to a beneficiary is often overlooked.[33]

2) A desired individual trustee has a life. Meaning, people whom most grantors or trustees would want to appoint as their successor trustee are typically successful, intelligent people with *full-time jobs*. Here the issue is less about experience, although it's still relevant, but more an issue of having the time or involvement to spend hours a month or even a week devoting precious time to the trustee's job. This often results in resignations and then further disruption to the original intention of the grantors.

3) Individuals rarely have a defined process of going about being trustee for a family. How are they making decisions? Are there beneficiaries who may take issue with those decisions? Are there bylaws? Typical individual trustees often accept the job because they care about the family personally, but because of the lack of professional experience on the administrative front, they may not necessarily make the best fiduciary. Without management, or most importantly, conflict avoidance and resolution skills, they can quickly become overwhelmed.

These reasons, among many, many others, make appointing a corporate trustee the preferred practice for a

---

[33] Trey T. Parker, Esq., "The Lesser-Known Duty to Inform and Report to Beneficiaries of a Trust," *WealthCounsel Quarterly* 6, no. 4 (October 2013), https://www.wealthcounsel.com/newsletter/Trey-Parker-The-Lesser-Known-Duty-to-Inform-and-Report-to-Beneficiaries-of-a-Trust.pdf.

family's governing documents. My preference is to have a corporate trustee named in a "successor co-trustee" role alongside a trustee's family or friend; in this way the personal aspects are still being captured by the governing documents.

Many advisors have shied away from using corporate trustees for fear of fees, bureaucratic obstacles, and faulty personnel—all of which I strongly agree are serious perils to the governing documents' role of adhering to the grantor's intentions. I have seen many a trust served by a corporate trustee that underwent five, ten, even fifteen organizational changes over twenty years due to mergers, acquisitions, or bank failures.

The solution that I propose is that families should engage an *independent, noncaptive corporate trustee advisor* skilled in the area of selecting from a variety of nonaffiliated corporate trustees for the family's specific goals and objectives. There are many independent broker/dealers working together with many noncaptive institutional trustees. Such an independent, corporate trustee advisor could also provide ongoing, independent review of the work the institution trustee is conducting for the family. This ongoing due diligence and independent oversight adds tremendous value to the family by providing solutions to the commonly perceived pitfalls of working directly with an institution without an intermediary.

A corporate trustee advisor would also have the ability to recommend, based on formal review reports and performance, a dismissal or termination of a serving institution. Then an alternate could be identified and appointed. I believe that most issues can be resolved with the corporate trustee once the intermediary advisor has identified the concern and the proposed solution, negotiating a fair and appropriate family-service outcome. A family's estate attorneys may also be able to make changes to governing documents that would allow for named corporate trustees to be dismissed and replaced with an alternate should the service or relationship become disadvantageous to the client family.[34]

Trust and estate attorneys rarely understand that a non-captive corporate trustee advisory service even exists in the financial-services industry. This book aims to be an effort in that education for attorneys and families alike.

---

[34] Robert A. Vigoda, Attorney, "Powers to Replace Trustees: A Key Element of (and Risk to) Dynasty Trusts," *Estate Planning* 35, no. 6 (June 2008), http://www.researchgate.net/publication/237597803_Powers_to_Replace_Trustees_A_Key_Element_of_(and_Risk_to)_Dynasty_Trusts_Empowering_beneficiaries_to_replace_trustees_may_safeguard_beneficiaries_from_an_entrenched_and_unresponsive_trustee._If_the_power_is_too_broad_however_it_threatens_to_undermine_the_long-term_preservation_of_family_wealth_contemplated_by_a_dynasty_trust.

CHAPTER NINE

How to Audit Your Broker

The distribution of investment products is all about making money for the product distributors and investment strategy manufacturers, under the promise and guise of generating profits for investors. I know this must come as a great shock, but suspend your disbelief for a moment.

Investors usually use two very distinct methods to purchase these investment products. The first is a discount or DIY platform, which encourages clients to sign up so that they may benefit from losing their money in a more pride-filled fashion while utilizing the "better tools, more graphs and charts, research ..." they so diligently provide. Why do retail investors think they can successfully conduct this work—make decisions, profitable ones at that, where they will make better deals versus the institutional players? The DIY providers sell snake oil—in the form of a false promise that cool-looking charts and graphs provide insight. It isn't the data that matter; it's the conclusions you draw from them that should drive competent decision making.

I believe that DIY investors choose this path not from a belief that they can do better than getting advice from institutions or FAs, but that rather, if someone is losing their money, it should be by their own doing. In this way an investor maintains a sense of control and ultimately knows that, at the very least, he or she has his or her own best interest at heart—essentially functioning as a self-fiduciary. But the more important question is: Is he or she the most-qualified person for this job?

The second major method of transacting in investments is via the wire-house brokerage firms who "broker" transactions. The primary fallacy is that brokers know something retail investors don't. In some ways this is true, but not in the area that investors prefer. Brokers are trained salespeople in the skill of financial product distribution, and the money-management industry (which creates the products they sell) spends hundreds of millions of dollars annually on that effort. The cost of the "education" of FAs is many, many tens of millions of dollars, sponsored by the self-serving interests of product manufacturers in a poorly disclosed practice called "revenue sharing."[35] I have many anecdotal stories from financial advisors who boldly claim gratitude to their mutual fund wholesalers, who've kept them in business over the years.

Brokers, and their firms, are compensated on the buying

---

[35] Leslie P. Norton, "When Fund Companies Pay to Play, So Do You," *Barron's*, April 12, 2014, http://online.barrons.com/articles/SB50001424053111904 223604579487610336424326.

and selling of securities of all varieties. When the brokerage houses also have investment banking operations, they are typically market makers too. A market maker does just that, provides an active trading facility for a particular security, often buying for their proprietary inventory in the process. Since these firms maintain an inventory of securities, they can then make sales directly to client accounts—a perfectly ready and underinformed retail buyer. Combine this function with a broker's portfolio construction proposal, and you have a perfect mechanism for inventory delivery. I don't mean to disparage this function of market making, but rather to encourage challenge and audit over the broker's motivations for making any trade recommendation.

The uncertainty surrounding these types of financial transactions and the high fees associated with the accounts lead many investors to choose DIY platforms. The most devastating experience is those investors who choose DIY platforms—fearful of neglect or failure of proper guidance at the hands of another—are happy (or more to the point, resigned) to suffer self-inflicted financial injury. How can this be as good as it gets? There are so many financial-services professionals available to the retail investor. American society has placed high ethical standards of care and high levels of trust into the hands of certain professionals—chiefly physicians and attorneys. Americans imbue these professionals with the highest level of respect and authority delegation. People put their faith and trust in those professionals. "I'll go to the doctor because I feel sick," or "I need an attorney to exact justice." Though I doubt anyone has actually uttered the latter, the intention behind it is that there's a professional who can give guidance in an area of specialized knowledge.

Why is it that the financial-services professional is perceived so differently from the aforementioned professionals of specialized knowledge? Could it be that the message being delivered by the financial sector is, by and large, that no such professional of specialized knowledge exists and that that knowledge is, in fact, democratized in access and interface? DIY investment platforms advertise: *"The Spirit of Independence … You Can Do This,"* and *"More Tools So You Can Dissect the Markets."* They are marketing to the same people who at most have dissected an earthworm in high school decades earlier. How can they expect the retail investor to traverse the treacherous and ever-changing ebbs and flows of the financial markets? Why would the DIY sector of the financial-services industry want to place the financial fate of millions of investors and billions of dollars into their untrained and emotionally charged hands? A patient would never choose to amputate his or her own leg; a defendant would not be readily admitted into court without the counsel of an attorney. Why is the financial-services industry not held to these same standards of care?

The answer is quite simple. Unlike those other professional industries, the financial-services arena, specifically broker/dealer firms and those selling investment-related products, is built on earning commissions on transactions. Brokers are paid very handsomely when investors flock to and flee from any security, be it stock, bond, or other. The more chaos, disorder, and panic, the better it is for these institutions' bottom line. Record profits are accrued at the individual's expense.

Investing is a market where someone must lose for another to gain on a per-transaction basis. Inherently this creates an adversarial system. This adversarial system is similar to the legal system, where Lady Justice is blind and the proverbial scales weigh the fate of the argument's victor. The "scales" of investing are the two opposed parties in the transaction. However, I believe that the one with a little more insight, perspective, and patience wins the investment return. Per our Mark Cuban quote earlier, every investor should ask before any transaction whether the opposing side of any transaction has better information or perspective on the investment opportunity. In reality, the odds are very, very high that the answer will often be "yes," especially since the other side of the transaction is often a massive institutional buyer or seller.

To narrow the information gap, one should seek counsel from a carefully researched and interrogated referral to a financial advisor. Be careful to weigh the advisor's recommendations in light of his or her *mode and duration* of compensation. A financial advisor who does not earn compensation based on client transactions would best serve most investors. A fee-based advisor who earns a living either by a percentage of client assets under management or a simple flat planning fee offers a better overall alignment of interests. But as we discussed, even within this type of remuneration, there can be conflicts of interests that reside within these relationships.

DECIDING TO HIRE (OR FIRE) YOUR FINANCIAL ADVISOR

Of the two methods just discussed, the financial advisor offers more for the investor than the DIY platforms. I've developed a series of investigative questions for hiring a financial advisor. Or if you already have an advisor, these questions can help audit the quality of the advice, performance, and any previously undisclosed conflicts. They may reveal concerns that lead you to a decision to seek out another advisor altogether. I've summarized the qualitative questioning into a checklist in the back of the book as well, so you can more easily use it. *Tear it out and take it along with you to your next interview meeting.* The qualitative questioning focuses on three main areas: compensation, accountability, and conflicts.

Compensation: Remember that how the broker is compensated can affect the products you're recommended to buy, which can then affect how your money performs. Red flags include compensation that incentivizes the placement of money with certain money managers instead of investing money where it is best for your goals and risk tolerance.

    a. *How are you compensated if I agree to this recommendation?* This should include any and all fees, commissions, or bonus pay related to the transaction. It should also include disclosure on whether the advisor will benefit from any kickbacks or marketing support dollars from the money-management solutions utilized.

b. *How do you know this recommendation is in my best long-term interest, and is your compensation and duty aligned with that time frame?* Advisors worth being hired will really enjoy this question, since it gives them an opportunity to articulate their specific value proposition and the wealth-care standard they provide.

Accountability: You can access the ADV forms (both parts) online, and it is a red flag if the *advisor* doesn't want to walk you through the forms. These forms will disclose any conflicts, as we discussed in chapters 4 and 7. Ask about total return and risk metrics (e.g., beta and alpha). Be sure you can see how well your money is performing relative to benchmark indices. It's best if your advisor uses the same indices to compare your portfolio performance to regularly.

c. *What factors are considered to measure portfolio management success or failure?* Allow the advisor to give you a full education on how they measure failure or success. Just because your portfolio is up in market value does not mean you are doing well. Conversely, a portfolio falling in value doesn't mean you're doing poorly.

d. *Do you provide performance tools or metrics that will show me whether I should fire you (e.g., performance relative to specific blended benchmarks)? Is there an investment policy statement governing your actions?* An investment policy statement (IPS) is a powerful portfolio governance tool. It will provide you and the advisor a common understanding of the goals and objectives that should be front of mind when choosing investments for the portfolio. A breach of the IPS should result in immediate termination. You should consider a probationary period for your advisor should the portfolio performance consistently underperform agreed-upon benchmarks given risk and return comparisons. After more than two years of underperformance based on risk/reward analysis, the advisor should be terminated.

e. *Who oversees and audits your advice?* Are there local branch supervisors reviewing investment decisions? With what frequency? What are these individuals' credentials, education, or qualifications? Can you sit down with the local (FINRA Series 24) Registered Principal to review the internal auditing procedures? Feel free to ask the compensation and accountability questions to the Registered Principal as well.

f. *Can I review ADV Forms Part 1 and 2?* Have them walk you through the conflicts-of-interest sections, as well as other eyebrow-raising provisions. It's better to have an advisor share with you the conflicts than to have one who hides the information or tries to minimize it.

Conflicts: As noted earlier, conflicts of interest, especially those revealed in Part 2 of the ADV form, affect the products you're offered and how well they perform. It may not be unusual to have some of these remunerations, but consider the source and how much it will influence your advisor.

g. *Do you receive any other financial or nonfinancial remuneration, including but not limited to marketing support dollars for client-appreciation events, seminars, dinners, golf outings, retreats, or conference trips, either from your own employer firm or any money manager/ product sponsor connected to the recommendation?* This delves deeper into the compensation realm with more specific detail.

h. *Do your recommendations come from a suitability- or fiduciary-care standard?* Have your advisor explain why they provide a particular service over another. Also, if they do provide fiduciary care, what kind? Is it the SEC version or the OCC version?

i. *Are there any proprietary or affiliated money managers in your recommendation?* Fairly self-explanatory, whose implications are poorly understood. The best advisor is one who avoids using any proprietary or affiliated money manager for your portfolio. This avoids even the appearance of conflicts.

j. *Can those funds be transferred in-kind easily to any other custodial platform?* Often the proprietary funds of one investment firm cannot be easily transferred to another firm. This results in major, unexpected realized long-term and short-term capital gains, adding tax consequence and liability.

Notice there is not one question that asks about historical performance, whether the broker owns the product in his or her own portfolio (do people even check?), or anything not relevant to the act of having been presented with a recommendation. Any investigation as to *why* is *this* particular recommendation being made to you at *this* precise moment in time is an attempt to root out any possible conflicts of interest. *Is it possible that a wholesaler from a money-management firm or his or her proprietary trading desk just took the broker to a fancy lunch, promised him or her more client seminar support, and this is why you're getting pitched this recommendation?*

CHAPTER TEN

Final Thoughts

As you can tell, the retail investor is not served well by the present system. The reality is that overall portfolio total return is overwhelmingly dictated by asset-class ownership.[36] FAs are not in the business of providing long-term investment success; they are more specifically in the business of providing a recommendation that in a moment of time happens to strike agreement with an underinformed investor, who filled out a clumsy, overgeneralizing risk-tolerance questionnaire to give the appearance of assessment.

Research like those cited in this chapter and from many an independent industry think tank shows that the most important contribution to portfolio total return is major asset allocation (e.g., how much stock, bond, and cash are held and in

---

[36] Gary P. Brinson, L. Randolph Hood, and Gilbert L. Beebower, "Determinants of Portfolio Performance," *Financial Analysts Journal*, January–February 1995, 133–138, http://www.cfapubs.org/doi/pdf/10.2469/faj.v51.n1.1869.

what proportion)—not the particular stock or fund that might be utilized. Also, behavioral finance studies have articulated that the primary emotions of fear and greed are irrational drivers of any investor's decision-making process.[37] This is one of the best things I learned from working for institutional money managers. Many of them continue to write extensively about investor behavior and how the typical outcome is at odds with the investor's desired results.

This emotional element alone is perilous for any investor working with a broker, since the broker is compensated solely by making the transaction and *not* by the *success* of the investment transaction. This is in contrast to a structure where advisors would be compensated solely based on the market value of the portfolio, in an ongoing small monthly percentage, as introduced earlier.

Thus the FA, in its broker role, can be a key destructor of wealth for families. He or she is an agent of change, enabling the euphoric or depressive lead of his or her client, not challenging the erroneous and herd mentality that is so prominently displayed and spewed in the business media. The legendary Benjamin Graham (another one of Warren Buffett's fabled mentors), regarded as the Father of Value Investing, discussed

[37] Jay R. Ritter, Cordell Professor of Finance, University of Florida, "Behavioral Finance," *Pacific-Basin Finance Journal* 11, no. 4 (September 2003): 429–437, http://bear.warrington.ufl.edu/ritter/publ_papers/Behavioral%20Finance.pdf.

that Mr. Market has always been fairly manic-depressive.[38] This rubs off on Mr. Market's investors.

To further the point of the challenges around FA behavior and recommendations, there was a poorly publicized publication from the National Bureau of Economic Research (NBER).[39] Its findings are cited here.

> Do financial advisors undo or reinforce the behavioral biases and misconceptions of their clients? We use an audit methodology where trained auditors meet with financial advisors and present different types of portfolios ... We document that advisors fail to de-bias their clients and often reinforce biases that are in *sic* [the financial advisors'] interests. Advisors encourage returns-chasing behavior and push for actively managed funds that have higher fees, even if the client starts with a well-diversified, low-fee portfolio.

This impressive paper is authored by not one, but three respected academics: Sendhil Mullainathan, Dept. of Economics at Harvard University; Markus Noeth, LS

---

[38] Benjamin Graham, *The Intelligent Investor: The Definitive Book on Value Investing. A Book of Practical Counsel—Revised Edition* (HarperCollins Publishers Inc., New York, NY, 1973).

[39] Sendhil Mullainathan, Markus Noeth, and Antoinette Schoar, *The Market for Financial Advice: An Audit Study*, NBER Working Paper No. 17929, Issued March 2012. Quote is from the Abstract on the Cover Page. http://www.nber.org/papers/w17929.

Banking & Behavioral Finance at University of Hamburg; and Antoinette Schoar, MIT Sloan School of Management. Their conclusions are clear and rational, having employed a controlled study. *TIME* magazine published an article discussing the disappointing findings from the NBER audit study.[40] However, there was little media coverage beyond this one reference.

Financial anxiety and euphoria are *good* for brokerage firms, as trading profits of most Wall Street firms still constitute a primary portion of total revenues. This is the very irony inherent in the industry. Advertise that you are a haven from the madness of Wall Street, as all major wire houses do, a sensible advisor in tumultuous times, only to truly make your money by doing exactly the opposite, thriving off the emotional thrusts of clients, knowing full well that revenues are only a market cycle away.

But this book is not about how to invest money. Nor is it about understanding economic theory. It's simply a chance to let investors and professional advisors alike have a bit more information than they did before with regard to their financial decision making and advisor selection.

The way to change something is not simply to denounce it, but to actively subvert it by being the solution you seek. It's in that spirit where I find myself at work today in the industry, believing ultimately that a better-educated consumer is a more successful one. If the words herein offer some greater fodder in

---

[40] Christopher Matthews, "Your Financial Adviser Might Be a Lemon," *TIME*, March 29, 2012, http://business.time.com/2012/03/29/your-financial-adviser-might-be-a-lemon/.

the consumer's fight to evolve the financial-services product dissemination paradigm into one with more retail investor benefit, then we will all ultimately prevail.

In my own way, I hope that this short book brings to the forefront a unique perspective that will enable a different kind of revolution than what my grandfather had endured—a revolution that empowers the retail investor with knowledge about how to identify which financial advisors are most aligned with their own interests, and in doing so, help them find themselves on a more profitable (because it's a conflict-free) investment path.

FOOTNOTES (IN NUMERICAL ORDER AS SUMMARY REFERENCE)

1   Jose M. Illán, *Cuba: Facts & Figures of an Economy in Ruins 1902–1963*, 1st ed. in English (Editorial ATP, Miami, FL, July 1964)—my grandfather's seminal publication on the subject. This citation is from the publisher on the back cover.

2   Diya Gullapalli, "A Fund That May Be Unforgettable: Pummeled Munder NetNet Haunts Firm's Turnaround," *Wall Street Journal*, October 3, 2006, http://online.wsj.com/articles/SB115921512811973383.

3   Stacy Forster, "InteractiveFunds, iExchange Merge, Plan a Mutual Fund," *Wall Street Journal*, October 22, 2000, http://www.wsj.com/articles/SB971969080654210587.

4   Tom Lauricella, "Online 'Community' Funds Aren't Finding Much Support," *Wall Street Journal*, April 2, 2001, C1, http://www.wsj.com/articles/SB986164214781499677.

5   Shawndra Hill and Noah Ready-Campbell, "Expert Stock Picker: The Wisdom of (Experts in) Crowds," *International Journal of Electronic Commerce* 15, no. 3 (Spring 2011): 73–102, http://www.researchgate.net/publication/228403831_Expert_Stock_Picker_The_Wisdom_of_(Experts_in)_Crowds.

6   Zach Anchors, "Table Gets Turned on a Panicked Client," Dow Jones Newswires, July 14, 2011, http://www.alignewealth.com/new/alignewealth/PracticeMgmt_DowJonesSMALL.pdf?advisorid=4022370.

7   Christopher B. Philips, CFA, and Francis M. Kinniry Jr., CFA, "Mutual Fund Ratings and Future Performance," Vanguard Research, June 2010, http://www.vanguard.com/pdf/icrwmf.pdf.

8   Anna Bernasek, "Choices Abound in an E.T.F. Boom," *New York Times*, July 12, 2014, http://www.nytimes.com/2014/07/13/business/mutfund/choices-abound-in-an-etf-boom.html?_r=0.

9   Chris Flood, "Underperformance Rife Among Active Fund Managers," *Financial Times Limited*, August 24, 2011, http://www.ft.com/intl/cms/s/0/d3b7db8e-ce5e-11e0-99ec-00144feabdc0.html#axzz3ZUTYpFdx.

10 Kelly Kearsley, "When a Client Has Multiple Financial Advisers," *Wall Street Journal*, December 20, 2013, http://www.wsj.com/articles/SB1000142405270230436720457927008148175880.

11 Roy Williams and Vic Pressier, *Preparing Heirs* (San Francisco: Robert D. Reed Publishers, 2003).

12 Barry James Dyke, *The Pirates of Manhattan* (Portsmouth, NH: 555 Publishing, 2007).

13 Joe Light, "And the Next Star Fund Manager Is ...," *Wall Street Journal*, January 17, 2014, http://www.wsj.com/articles/SB10001424052702304419104579324871451038920.

14 Prof. Richard Ebeling, "Free Market Capitalism vs. Crony Capitalism," *EPICTimes*, July 14, 2014, http://www.epictimes.com/2014/07/free-market-capitalism-vs-crony-capitalism/.

15 "The Stock Market Is Still for Suckers and Why You Should Put Your Money in the Bank," The Mark Cuban Weblog, August 20, 2010, http://blogmaverick.com/2010/08/20/the-stock-market-is-still-for-suckers-and-why-you-should-put-your-money-in-the-bank/.

16 Sebastian Schich, "Insurance Companies and the Financial Crisis," *OECD Journal: Financial Market Trends* 2009, no. 2 (October 2009), http://www.oecd.org/finance/financial-markets/44260382.pdf.

17 Peter Coy, "Alexander Hamilton Was Even More Amazing Than You Thought," *Bloomberg Businessweek—Global Economics*, May 9, 2014, http://www.businessweek.com/articles/2014-05-09/alexander-hamilton-was-even-more-amazing-than-you-thought.

18 Ann Saphir, "With the End of Fed's QE in Sight, U.S. Public Says 'Huh?'" Reuters, September 17, 2013, http://www.reuters.com/article/2013/09/17/us-usa-fed-poll-idUSBRE98G18K20130917.

19 *FINRA 2013 Year in Review and Annual Financial Report*, FINRA, 2014, https://www.finra.org/file/finra-2013-year-review-and-annual-financial-report.

20 Liz Skinner, "FINRA Reports Dramatic Jump in Restitution in 2012," *Investment News*, January 8, 2013, http://www.investmentnews.com/article/20130108/FREE/130109952/finra-reports-dramatic-jump-in-restitution-in-2012.

21 Gary Rivlin, "How Wall Street Defanged Dodd-Frank," *Nation*, May 20, 2013. Gary Rivlin is an Investigative Fund reporting fellow at the Nation Institute, http://www.thenation.com/article/174113/how-wall-street-defanged-dodd-frank.

22 Barry R. Temkin and Michael R. Koblenz, "New Suitability and Fiduciary Standards for Financial Advisers Under the Wall Street Reform Act and FINRA Rules," *Securities Arbitration Commentator* 2010, no. 2 (March 2011), http://www.moundcotton.com/sites/default/files/NewSuitabilityAndFiduciaryStandards.pdf.

23 Allan Chernoff, Sr. Correspondent, CNN, "Madoff Whistleblower Blasts SEC" February 4, 2009. This report includes the following quote: "A fraud investigator told Congress that he'd warned the agency about Madoff's Ponzi scheme years ago. But his efforts went nowhere." http://money.cnn.com/2009/02/04/news/newsmakers/madoff_whistleblower/.

24 Daisy Maxey, "For Many Auction-Rate Investors, the Freeze Goes On," *Wall Street Journal*, March 13, 2012, http://www.wsj.com/articles/SB10001424052970203960804577243554110930094.

25 Justin Lahart, "Maybe This Is Why the Stock Market Gets Called a Casino ..." *Wall Street Journal*, November 4, 2013, http://blogs.wsj.com/economics/2013/11/04/maybe-this-is-why-the-stock-market-gets-called-a-casino/.

26 Section 202(a)(11)(D) of the Investment Advisors Act of 1940, As Amended Through P.L. 112-90, Approved January 3, 2012, https://www.sec.gov.about/laws/iaa40.pdf.

27 Regulation 194—Frequently Asked Questions—11 NYCRR 30 (Regulation 194), http://www.dfs.ny.gov/insurance/faqs/faqs-reg194.htm.

28 Edward Siedle, Contributor, "The Greatest Retirement Crisis in American History," Forbes.com, March 20, 2013, http://www.forbes.com/sites/edwardsiedle/2013/03/20/the-greatest-retirement-crisis-in-american-history/.

29 Jordan Maglich, Contributor, "A Ponzi Pandemic: 500+ Ponzi Schemes Totaling $50Billion in 'Madoff Era,'" *Forbes Magazine*, February 12, 2014, http://www.forbes.com/sites/jordanmaglich/2014/02/12/a-ponzi-pandemic-500-ponzi-schemes-totaling-50-billion-in-madoff-era/.

30 Thomas Forrest, CPA, AEP, "How a Corporate Trustee Can Help a Financial Planner Meet Their Client's Goals," *Journal of Financial Service Professionals* 61, no. 6 (November, 2007), https://www.naepc.org/journal/issue06g.pdf.

31 For a variety of studies on the subject of behavioral finance, Yale School of Management and the International Center for Finance have an excellent resource center, found at http://som.yale.edu/faculty-research/our-centers/international-center-finance/research-initiatives/behavioral-finance.

32 Madeline Vann, MPH, "Managing Stress in Tough Economic Times," Medically reviewed by Cynthia Haines, MD, *Everyday Health*, December 22, 2009, http://www.everydayhealth.com/emotional-health/managing-stress-in-bad-economy.aspx.

33 Trey T. Parker, Esq., "The Lesser-Known Duty to Inform and Report to Beneficiaries of a Trust," *WealthCounsel Quarterly* 6, no. 4 (October 2013), https://www.wealthcounsel.com/newsletter/Trey-Parker-The-Lesser-Known-Duty-to-Inform-and-Report-to-Beneficiaries-of-a-Trust.pdf.

34 Robert A. Vigoda, Attorney, "Powers to Replace Trustees: A Key Element of (and Risk to) Dynasty Trusts," *Estate Planning* 35, no. 6 (June 2008), http://www.researchgate.net/publication/237597803_Powers_to_Replace_Trustees_A_Key_Element_of_(and_Risk_to)_Dynasty_Trusts_Empowering_beneficiaries_to_replace_trustees_may_safeguard_beneficiaries_from_an_entrenched_and_unresponsive_trustee._If_the_power_is_too_broad_however_it_threatens_to_undermine_the_long-term_preservation_of_family_wealth_contemplated_by_a_dynasty_trust.

35 Leslie P. Norton, "When Fund Companies Pay to Play, So Do You," *Barron's*, April 12, 2014, http://online.barrons.com/articles/SB50001424053111904223604579487610336424326.

36 P. Brinson, L. Randolph Hood, and Gilbert L. Beebower, "Determinants of Portfolio Performance," *Financial Analysts Journal*, January–February

1995, 133–138, http://www.cfapubs.org/doi/pdf/10.2469/faj.v51.n1.1869.

37 Jay R. Ritter, Cordell Professor of Finance, University of Florida, "Behavioral Finance," *Pacific-Basin Finance Journal* 11, no. 4 (September 2003): 429–437, http://bear.warrington.ufl.edu/ritter/publ_papers/Behavioral%20Finance.pdf.

38 Benjamin Graham, *The Intelligent Investor: The Definitive Book on Value Investing. A Book of Practical Counsel—Revised Edition* (HarperCollins Publishers Inc., New York, NY, 1973).

39 Sendhil Mullainathan, Markus Noeth, and Antoinette Schoar, *The Market for Financial Advice: An Audit Study*, NBER Working Paper No. 17929, Issued March 2012. Quote is from the Abstract on the Cover Page. http://www.nber.org/papers/w17929.

40 Christopher Matthews, "Your Financial Adviser Might Be a Lemon," *TIME*, March 29, 2012, http://business.time.com/2012/03/29/your-financial-adviser-might-be-a-lemon/.

GLOSSARY

ADV, as in ADV Forms Part 1 and Part 2. The abbreviation is probably short for *Advisor Disclosure and Verification*, but nowhere is it clearly explained. This is a disclosure document that clients should request to be reviewed prior to hiring an advisor. Both individual advisor reps (IARs) and firms (RIAs) will have ADVs that can be delivered on demand. These documents contain valuable information on the people, organization, fees, and conflicts that may exist.

Broker/Dealers are firms that employ FINRA-registered representatives (who hold Series 6, 7, etc. licenses) that buy and sell securities for clients, either as agents (on behalf of clients) or as dealers (a.k.a. principals) when trading their own account assets. This is the old-fashioned world of stockbrokers, who call up clients and pitch a stock, mutual fund, or other product for sale to generate commissions. Confusion exists for many clients when they believe they have a financial advisor, who is really only providing the recommendations of a broker.

When the institution trades for itself, it's a dealer. When it trades on behalf of a customer, it's a broker.

Conflict of Interest (COI) occurs when other advisor motivations exist during a product sale or investment recommendation, including factors not related to the client's interests, such as commissions, promised marketing support, or special bonuses.

Corporate Trustee, a.k.a. institutional trustee, is an entity that serves clients with the regulatory oversight and duties of a fiduciary-care standard. However, self-serving agendas in the form of proprietary products—which should be avoided—may show up in their services.

Discounters or DIY service providers offer the services to trade for a fee that's lower than a full-service broker, but they don't provide customized financial advice.

Distribution channel is the mechanism by which money-management firms sell their products to investing clients. There are many channels, such as wire houses, independents, RIAs, and banks. These firms work in close partnership with the money manager product manufacturers to maximize profit in selling to client investors.

Fiduciary is an individual or entity that is entrusted with managing the assets of another to solely deliver results that are in the other's best interest, while avoiding self-serving agendas.

Financial Advisor (FA) is an umbrella term that refers to someone who advises you about your financial investments. However, it is a generic term with little meaning or description as to the service conveyed by the provider.

Financial industry regulators—included for the discussion herein are Financial Industry Regulatory Authority (FINRA), the Securities and Exchange Commission (SEC), and the Office of the Comptroller of the Currency (OCC) regulators. Each entity has specific standards of care, ranging from low-level suitability standards that brokers and advisors adhere to from FINRA, to the disclosure-acceptable fiduciary standard from the SEC, to the OCC's fiduciary entity standard, which allows firms to serve as trustees for families.

Investment Advisor Representative (IAR) is an individual who gives advice on investing in securities such as stocks, bonds, mutual funds, or exchange-traded funds. Mainly compensated through fees based upon assets under management. They are required to disclose any conflicts of interests, but few do so in plain English.

Registered Investment Advisors (RIAs) as investment providers are quite different from the broker/dealer product distribution model. RIAs are more about being the product itself—a money manager, who then manufactures investment solutions that are often distributed through distribution channels. The Securities and Exchange Commission defines RIAs as individuals or firms that are registered with the SEC and in the business of giving advice about securities. They are paid by percentage of assets they manage, an hourly fee, a fixed fee, or a commission, if the advisor is also a broker/dealer. There are many independent RIAs that do not manufacture products, but rather manage client funds in a specific strategy or mandate.

Suitability is a standard of care provided by FINRA and its agents or brokers. It deems that recommendations and advice must be appropriate at the *time* of the recommendation based upon client needs, objectives, and risk tolerances. There is no requirement to provide ongoing monitoring and advice on the product or investment after the sale is made.

Wholesalers represent the packaged products of investment management manufacturers and sell to distribution channels and their reps. A national sales manager is typically in charge of many dozens of external wholesalers and internal wholesalers scattered across the country. Managing director and vice president are common titles for external wholesalers who are based in the field with specific geographic coverage. Internal wholesalers are often located in a central location to provide ongoing broad-based coverage and communications with the various distribution channels. These channels were broken into several subsets like those introduced at the book's opening, including the largest broker/dealers within the wirehouse, regional, independent, and registered investment advisor (RIA) markets.

Wire houses are also known as full-service broker/dealers. They provide financial advice as well as the services needed to trade and invest, but the commissions are higher. Wire-house firms are just the most popular broker/dealer firms for investments. There used to be many, many more wire-house firms, but the Big 4 are now Merrill Lynch, Morgan Stanley, UBS, and Wells Fargo. Wire-house brokers got their name from the late 1800s because they leased dedicated telegraph lines to transmit financial data more quickly.

THE *HOW TO HIRE (OR FIRE) YOUR FINANCIAL ADVISOR* CHECKLIST

Red Flags: If the FA talks about a new product available just minutes into your first interview, just cut the meeting short. If he or she shares any charts or fund-performance information at any time during the initial interview, don't bother hiring him or her. If the FA isn't excited about the opportunity to provide you with transparency in his or her compensation and conflicts, keep on looking at other candidates.

Questions:

1) How are you compensated if I agree to this recommendation?
2) How do you know this recommendation is in my best long-term interest, and is your compensation and duty aligned with that time frame?
3) What factors are considered to measure portfolio management success or failure?
4) Do you provide performance tools or metrics that will show me whether I should fire you (e.g., performance relative to specific blended benchmarks)? Is there an investment policy statement governing your actions?
5) Who oversees and audits your advice?
6) Can I review ADV Forms Part 1 and 2?
7) Do you receive any other financial or nonfinancial remuneration, including but not limited to marketing support dollars for client-appreciation events, seminars, dinners, golf outings, retreats, or conference trips, either

from your own employer firm or any money manager/ product sponsor connected to the recommendation?

8) Do your recommendations come from a suitability- or fiduciary-care standard?

9) Are there any proprietary or affiliated money managers in your recommendation?

10) Can those funds be transferred in-kind easily to any other custodial platform?

NOTES

NOTES

NOTES

NOTES

INDEX

W

Wall Street, versus Main Street, 59–60

The Wall Street Journal, 5, 11

Wall Street Reform and Consumer Production Act, 52

Wealth transfer, 23

Wedbush Morgan, 33

Wells Fargo, 33

Wholesalers
    definition, 102

description, 34–36

Wire-house broker/dealers, 32–33, 78–79

Wire houses, 32–33
    definition, 103

24838817R00082

Made in the USA
San Bernardino, CA
08 October 2015